C000273914

heavenly BEER

"The good Lord has changed water into wine,
so how can drinking beer be a sin?"

*sign in the café de vrede,
opposite the westvleteren monastery
and brewery in Belgium.*

heavenly BEER

Roger Protz

CARROLL & BROWN PUBLISHERS LIMITED

heavenly beer

was created and produced by
CARROLL & BROWN LIMITED
20 Lonsdale Road
Queen's Park
London NW6 6RD

Editor **Tom Broder**
Managing Art Editor **Emily Cook**
Managing Editors **Becky Alexander, Michelle Bernard**
Photography **Jules Selmes**

Text copyright © 2002 Roger Protz
Copyright illustrations and compilation
© 2002 Carroll & Brown Limited

A CIP catalogue record for this book is available
from the British Library

ISBN 1-903258-46-4

Reproduced by Emirates, Dubai
Printed and bound by Ajanta, India
First Edition

All rights reserved.

No part of this publication may be reproduced in any material form (including
photocopying or storing it in any medium by electronic means and whether or not
transiently or incidentally to some other use of this publication) without the written
permission of the copyright owner, except in accordance with the provisions of the
Copyright, Designs and Patents Act of 1988 or under the terms of a licence issued by
the Copyright Licensing Agency, 90 Tottenham Court Road, London W1P 9HE.
Applications for the copyright owner's written permission to reproduce any part
of this publication should be addressed to the publisher.

contents

introduction

chapter 1 **The beers**

chapter 2 **Enjoying beer**

introduction

Beer is the oldest and most widespread of the world's alcoholic drinks, with origins that stretch back thousands of years before the birth of Christ. But it was the monks of the medieval Church who adopted the brewing of beer most enthusiastically, and the decline of the monastic way of life has not diminished the modern-day influence of these brewing monks. From the early Middle Ages through to the present day, monks have been crafting full-flavoured, tasty beers in the calm of their abbey cloisters.

This introductory chapter examines the long and fertile history of monastic brewing. It explores how – and why – the monks made beer, and how medieval ingredients and brewing methods produced the unique and stimulating flavours that modern brewers are only now learning to fully appreciate and imitate.

monastic BReWiNg

Daybreak in the Middle Ages: a monk rises from his cot in a humble cell, covers his tonsured head in a warm cowl, and hurries to chapel to celebrate matins. It is an image deeply ingrained in history, one that has been handed down to modern times.

What is less well-known is that – at a time when the Church dominated and controlled people's lives throughout the Christian world – some monks with special duties and skills would rise from their beds to fire mash tuns and coppers, and make ale for their communities. Even today, in a few surviving monasteries, monks still go quietly about the business of making beer to sustain their brothers, and to raise funds to support their ministry and maintain their abbeys. The bonds between Church and brewing have a long – and remarkably fertile – history.

the BiRth oF BReWiNg

Beer is the world's oldest and most widely consumed alcoholic drink. Its origins lie in Ancient Egypt, Babylonia and Mesopotamia. Growing grain to make beer and bread turned nomads into settlers 3,000 years before the birth of Christ. In the first millennium BC, as Phoenician sea-faring traders took both cereals and the knowledge of beer-making to other

countries, the art of brewing also established itself in northern Europe. The spread of Islam across North Africa and the Middle East in the 7th and 8th century AD, however, meant severe restrictions were placed on alcohol and this helped to retard the further development of brewing in the birthplace of beer. But the genie was out of the bottle. Across the wheat and barley growing regions of northern Europe, beer had established itself at the very heart of society: a position it retains today.

A PAGAN BREW

When the Roman armies marched northwards across Europe, they were impressed by the natives' ability to make alcohol from grain and to store it in wooden casks. The wine-drinking Romans were less impressed with the taste of ale, but the Germanic tribes that took control of parts of Northern Europe, the British Isles and Scandinavia had cultures steeped in drinking: variations on the word *öl* developed into ale, a term that for centuries indicated a cereal-based drink made without hops. Another Saxon word for ale, *woet*, survives today as wort, the term for the sweet sugary extract produced by mixing malt with water.

ANGLO-SAXON ALES

Anglo-Saxon life was punctuated by frequent bouts of ale drinking. Feasts, weddings and burials were all excuses for making and

Liquid bread

Ale was central to monastic life. It was consumed with the frugal meals of the monks and was considered a vital part of their diets. While abbots and bishops began to accumulate considerable wealth and power, the life of the average monk was one of grinding poverty and drudgery, alleviated only by a few tankards of nutritious ale for breakfast, lunch and supper alongside bread, thin vegetable soup and, when their luck was in, cheese. Vitamins of the B-family, present in ale, played a key role in keeping drinkers healthy. The consumption of ale was especially important during Lent, the time of fasting that lasts for 40 days between Ash Wednesday and Easter. The term 'liquid bread' was coined by monks to stress the way in which ale sustained them during the period that mirrored Christ's fasting in the wilderness.

"He who drinks
beer sleeps well.

He who sleeps well
cannot sin.

He who does not
sin goes to heaven.

Amen."

18th century
german beer stein

consuming vast amounts of alcohol. In the Anglo-Saxon period, brewing was a domestic process: it was as natural for the woman of the house to make ale as it was to make bread. She was, after all, using common ingredients for both. Gradually, the best female brewers, known as brewsters or ale-wives, began to offer their drinks to people outside their homes: it was during this period that the ale house or 'public house' began to develop.

Stories of the prodigious drinking habits of the Anglo-Saxons and their Viking counterparts are probably exaggerated. They could not have conquered vast areas, built towns and villages, and raised crops and animals – as well as engaging in the odd bout of rape and pillage – if they had been in a perpetual state of bestial drunkenness. More likely, they drank ale because it was the only safe thing to do at a time when water and milk were dangerous and even lethal. It served the purpose of the early Christians to paint a portrait of a dissolute way of life before their saintly arrival.

holy guardians

The church was keen to stamp its total authority on society by controlling pleasure as well as prayer. The income from ale was also not lost on abbots. Ale was sold to pilgrims, if they had the wherewithal, and also was used as a form of barter and for the payment of tolls, rents and debts. In AD 852, for example, a man

The Abbey of St. Gall

Ruins of an early brewhouse at St. Gall, in Switzerland, provide the earliest surviving layout of a medieval brewery in Europe. The abbey, founded in AD 613 by an Irish monk, St. Gall, included a malt house, a kiln for curing malt, a mill room for grinding malt, and no less than three breweries and storage cellars. It seems that the abbey adopted the method of producing three separate types of ale: the best ale, made with the best-quality grain, was reserved for those at the very top of the clerical hierarchy.

known only as Wulfrud rented land from the Abbot of Medeshampstede (which became the modern English city of Peterborough) in exchange for two tuns – giant casks – of ale a year. The church's power stretched beyond the cloisters. Theodore, Archbishop of Canterbury in the 7th century AD, decreed that if a Christian layman drank too much, he would have to face a 15-day penance.

DRUNK MONKS

The amount of ale each monk could consume was also strictly regulated and was usually in the order of eight pints of weak ale per day. Drunkenness was frowned upon. In the 6th century, St. Gildas the Wise decreed that any monk whose speech was too thick to sing the evening psalms coherently would have to forfeit his supper. A novice monk, tricked by elder brethren into drinking too much ale, had to do 15 days' penance. A more experienced brother found in a state of inebriation would be given 40 days' penance.

BREWING BROTHERS

The Church not only laid down the law where consumption was concerned but also cornered the market in terms of production. While the Abbot of Medeshampstede may have been content to get his supplies in lieu of rent, many monasteries built their own brewhouses. Pilgrims were offered accommodation at monasteries, and inns were built alongside for poorer pilgrims who were not allowed to eat in close proximity to the abbots. Some monasteries had three separate brewhouses: one produced the finest quality ale for the distinguished visitors and senior monks; a second made weaker ale for ordinary monks and lay employees; a third, usually in an inn or almonry, brewed cheap ale for impoverished pilgrims who sought bed and board.

were sometimes so thick that they had to be diluted with water. As the dregs contained a deposit of yeast, the unappetising brew was probably highly nutritious.

the discovery of hops

The Church was also involved – usually in a reactionary way – in the shift from ale to beer. In the Middle Ages, there was a sharp divide between the two styles, a rather different distinction to that commonly made today. Beer then referred to a brew containing hops. Ale was a strong drink made from grain and flavoured with all manner of herbs, plants and spices, including bog myrtle, cinnamon, cloves, ginger, ivy, laurel, nettles, rosemary and yarrow, to balance the sweetness of the malt.

A BITTER BREW

Records show that hops were grown in Babylon thousands of years before Christ. Ironically, although the Romans in Britain grew hops and ate them like asparagus, they did not pass them on to the native Celts, who made an unhopped ale called *curmi*. It was only during the great migration of people that followed the break-up of the Roman empire that knowledge of the hop's role in brewing was introduced into the Caucasus and parts of Germany by the Slavs.

Hops probably began to be used in brewing in Europe from the 8th century. Brewers quickly discovered the almost magical qualities of the

SOUR ALE AND BEER DREGS

Monasteries and abbeys with less space had just one brewhouse that would produce three strengths and qualities of ale by mashing, boiling and fermenting the same batch of grain three times. The weakest ale was given to nursing mothers and children as well as to pilgrims: this type of thin alcohol was immortalised by Shakespeare as 'small beer'. The quality of the weak ale left much to be desired. A 13th-century writer, describing the poverty of the Franciscans when they first settled in London in 1224, commented: 'I have seen the brothers drink ale so sour that some would have preferred to drink water.' He described how the friars took it in turns to sup the dregs of beer heated over the fire. The dregs

"I will make it felony to drink small beer"

shakespeare, henry vi, part 2

hop that set it apart from other plants. Hop resins include acids and tannins that give an enticing aroma to beer and a quenching bitterness, but the resins also prevent bacterial infection. Adding hops, especially when water was insanitary, became a vital stage of the brewing process. Early hop gardens were recorded in the Hallertau region of Bavaria in AD 736, and hop cultivation was chronicled in Prague at the same time. In 1079 the Abbess Hildegarde of Bingen, in Germany, referred in her writings to the use of hops in brewing.

CHURCH RESISTANCE

In every region, the hop had to fight a war of attrition with the old methods of brewing. Entrenched interests, usually controlled by the Church, resisted the hop. The mixture of plants, spices and herbs used to flavour beer before hops prevailed was known as gruit, and the supply of gruit was largely in the hands of the Church. In Cologne, the archbishop had cornered the gruit market through a decree called the *Grutrecht*; to defend his income he attempted to outlaw the use of hops. In Russia, Archduke Vassili II banned the use of the plant altogether. As early as the 14th century, the Dutch showed a craving for hopped German beer – importing thousands of barrels every year – but the Church continued to insist that the local ale be made with gruit. In England, where hops did not arrive until the 15th century,

they were banned in Norwich, while the burghers of Shrewsbury prohibited the 'wicked and pernicious weed'.

THE POPULAR CHOICE

Increasingly though, the common brewers offered hopped beer rather than ale. This made commercial sense, for beer had far better keeping qualities, was preferred by customers, and less malt was needed in a production process increasingly dominated by the profit motive. Some French monks may have followed suit, but most churches, for reasons of conservatism, isolation or ignorance, continued to make a style that was in terminal decline.

Bless the beer

Monks would mark their casks with crosses to denote the strength of each brew and as a benediction: the more crosses, the stronger the beer and, presumably, the greater the need for God's blessing. The habit survives today, with beers such as Greene King's XX Dark Mild.

how the monks made beer

With the medieval brewhouse lacking much of the technology and expertise that we take for granted today, the medieval brewer had to use all his ingenuity to produce a tasty ale for his brethren.

One of the most detailed studies of medieval monastic brewing that we have today is based on brewing in France (written in 1969 by Urion and Eyer). The ale was known as *cervoise*, from the Latin *cerevisia,* and it was made with a range of grains, including barley, oats, rye and wheat. Barley was preferred as it was easier to transform into malt – the starchy, germinated, dried grain vital to brewing.

step one

Grain was laid out in a cool cellar and moistened with water to encourage germination. In some breweries, the grain was spread on the ground overnight in secluded spots away from the wind so that the morning dew would moisten it. The malt was turned by hand to aerate it and stop the grains from tangling. When it started to sprout, the malt was moved to a stone-built kiln and laid out on a thin floor covered with hair cloth above a hearth. The progress of the transformation of barley into malt was tested by chewing it.

step two

Malt, with some unmalted cereal, was ground, and then placed in a mashing vessel, and mixed with hot water. The mash was stirred with a *fourquet* or mashing fork, and more water was added at increasingly higher temperatures until the mash was hot enough for saccharification to take place (the change of starch into maltose by natural enzymes in the malt). The brewer knew when this stage had been reached by simply placing his fork in the middle of the vat until the water began to simmer near the handle.

step three

The sweet liquid, called 'wort', was cooled, run into wooden vessels called tuns, and mixed with yeast. When fermentation was complete, the cervoise stood for several more days while a secondary fermentation turned remaining sugars into alcohol, and unwanted protein and dead yeast cells sank to the bottom of the vessels. The strength of the finished ale was surprisingly modest, between 4–6% abv.

Brewing Developments

Urion and Eyer also describe the brewing of
beer at a later date, when hops were used as an
integral part of the brewing process. By now,
mash tuns had a slotted base so that the spent
grain acted as a filter as the wort passed
through to a collecting vessel known as the
'under-back'. Hops were also added to the mash
tun as part of the filtering process. Brewers felt

Yeast: God's secret helper

Little is said about yeast in medieval descriptions of brewing.
The reason is simple: yeast was a mystery and remained so
until Pasteur unlocked its secrets in the 19th century. The
English called yeast 'God-is-Good': they thought the violent
fermentation and the creation of alcohol were the work of God.

The risk of infection from wild yeasts meant that brewing did
not take place in the summer months, when temperatures
could not be controlled. Monks would make special March
beers that would be stored and drunk during the summer until
cooler weather enabled brewing to start afresh, using the first
malts and hops of the new harvest. This ancient ritual is
celebrated today by the annual Munich Oktoberfest.

It seems certain, however, that brewers learned to avoid
spontaneous fermentation from wild yeasts in the air. To make
the beer as consistent as possible, yeast was collected from
one brew, carefully stored, and used for the next one.

that hops produced a better extract from the malt and also acted as a preservative.

The sweet extract was pumped back into the mash tun and filtered a second time to wash out any remaining malt sugars. The wort was then boiled with hops, with a short boil for light-coloured beers, and a longer one for a darker beer, a process that caused some of the sugar to caramelize. The wort was then cooled and fermented in the same fashion as cervoise.

The discovery of lager

It was in 15th-century Munich, a city founded by monks, that the first faltering steps were made to make beer by the lagering method – one of the great innovations in brewing history. The process was discovered by the Bavarian monks, quite by accident, during attempts to store beer in icy Alpine caves.

The cold storage caused some yeasts to change character. Rather than collecting at the top of the liquid in a thick, crusty froth, reacting with the warm air, the yeast sank to the bottom of the wort, fermenting more slowly. This produced a smoother, cleaner beer which could be stored for much longer periods – the word *lager* comes from the German 'to store'. Natural icy cellars can still be found in many of Bavaria's old monasteries and brewhouses.

Lagering on a commercial scale was not made possible until the development of modern refrigeration, guaranteeing cold temperatures throughout the year. The new lager beers were first popularized in the 19th century, by the Spaten brewery in Munich (see pages 70–71).

what did early Beers taste like?

The ingredients and brewing methods of the medieval period created flavours that only a few modern breweries seek to imitate, flavours that seem strange yet stimulating to the modern palate.

It is very difficult to be certain what early monastic beers tasted like. Recipes have not survived, if they existed at all. Until the Renaissance most people were illiterate and recipes were probably handed down by word of mouth. While many monks were able to read and write (their manuscripts are testimony to this), the brothers detailed to make ale were not necessarily similarly educated.

There are several surviving ancient beer styles: the lambic and gueuze ales of the Payottenland area around Brussels allow wild yeasts to impregnate the wort; the sahti beers of rural Finland use juniper rather than hops; and there are the porridge beers and bread beers of Africa and Russia. But these are idiosyncratic styles, particular to individual regions, and offer few clues as to what monks were brewing in the seclusion of their cloisters. Despite this, we can deduce much about how the early beers would have tasted from the ingredients and methods known to have been used by early brewers.

A RANDOM ELEMENT

Yeast picks up flavours from one brew and retains them for the next, giving each beer its own particular 'taste print' and house style. Before the 19th century, one batch of yeast might have had a dozen or more competing strains, some of which would impart undesirable flavours to the ale. Following work by Emil Christian Hansen in the Carlsberg Laboratories in Copenhagen, yeast cultures today are selected to use only the best strains, meaning the taste can be better controlled.

STORAGE

Ales and beers in the Middle Ages were often stored for long periods – as much as a year or more – in giant wooden casks known as tuns. The casks were unlined and wild yeasts could impregnate the maturing beer, while micro-organisms in the wood would also attack the liquid. From descriptions of the early porter beers brewed in London in the 18th century and stored in this fashion, as well as from the 'sour red' beers still made in the West Flanders region of Belgium, we know that such beers have a slightly sour and lactic flavour that most modern drinkers would find unacceptable.

WARM FERMENTING

Most ales during the monastic period would have been warm-fermented, a method that gives rich, fruity aromas and flavours, rarely found in

THE FLAVOUR OF SMOKE

Throughout the period of monastic dominance, malt would be made using wood-fuelled fires, rather than the coke or gas used today. Only during the Industrial Revolution of the 18th century, when coke (coal without the gases) was made, did it became possible to cure malt in kilns fired by coke. Malt cured by wood fires would have had a smoky character and was brown in colour, unlike today's pale malt.

MYSTERY INGREDIENTS

For most of the monastic period, ale was flavoured with herbs, plants and spices. From the little information that has survived, it is clear that monks used whatever ingredients were at hand, with barley being supplemented by wheat, oats, rye and other cereals. The character of the local water also played an important role in the taste of ale and beer, with breweries being attracted to areas with a supply of good spring water.

> "The selling of bad beer is a crime against Christian love"
>
> 13th c. law in the city of Augsburg

today's lager beers. Although attempts to store beer at low temperatures in icy caves in the Alps date from the 15th century, lagering on a commercial scale was made possible only by ice-making machines invented towards the end of the 19th century.

how monastery beers taste today

The ales made by the Trappist breweries in Belgium should not be perceived as derivatives of earlier monastic brews. Today's Trappist beers are magnificent – some of the world's classics – but it would be misleading to suggest they have anything in common with the monastic beers of the Middle Ages.

In San Francisco in the 1980s and in Britain in the 1990s, fascinating attempts were made to recreate the beers from Ancient Egypt and Mesopotamia using coriander, dates and honey in place of hops. Frustratingly, as a result of the inscriptions left by the people of the Old World, we have more information about beer from that period than from the far more recent one of medieval Europe. But there have been attempts to brew a medieval beer. For example, the King Cnut Ale brewed by the St. Peter's Brewery in England (see page 88) uses no hops, and instead uses stinging nettles. Allowing for modern varieties of cereals, water and yeast, this is a fascinating attempt to call up monastic beer as it might have been brewed in the past.

A taste of history

The work of the Haarlems Jopenbier brewery in the Netherlands may come close to giving a glimpse – and no more – of the taste of beer from the Middle Ages. Jopen Hoppenbier is brewed with barley malt, wheat, oats and hops, and is based on a 1501 recipe – thought to be the first beer brewed in Haarlem using hops. It is pale in colour, and has a sherry-like fruit aroma with spicy hops and creamy oats in the mouth. The finish becomes dry with a good balance of malt and hops.

Koyt – based on a recipe of 1407 – uses the mix of herbs and spices known as gruit. Oats are used as well as barley malt, while the gruit is composed principally of myrica (wax myrtle bark). The beer has a cloudy russet colour and a rich malt and spice aroma. The palate is tart, bitter and spicy, with a long finish with vinous malt, spices, herbs and a touch of lactic sourness. Frustratingly, the Dutch authorities insist that the beer must be made with hops. Without them, the beer would surely come close to giving us a taste of ancient times.

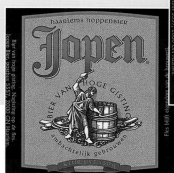

the Decline of monastic Brewing

The weakening power of the medieval Church spelt an end to the monastic dominance of brewing, with monasteries across Europe marginalized or dissolved. But even today, a few brewers continue to maintain the venerable traditions.

The 14th century was a decisive time for the Church. The Black Death ravaged Europe; entire communities were destroyed and the casualty rate was appalling. Around one-third of the population of Europe died and it took two centuries before the number of people was restored to a level predating the arrival of the plague from Asia. The Church, with its huge army of monks, was especially hard hit. So many priests died that the Pope decreed that laymen could administer the last rites to the dying. As a result, the Church's iron grip on society was weakened beyond repair.

power to the people

A shortage of clergy made it impossible for abbeys and churches to meet the needs of the whole population, either for beer or for spiritual refreshment, and commercial or 'common' brewers appeared everywhere to sell beer through inns and taverns. In other ways, too, the Church never fully recovered from the blow inflicted by the Black Death. As the Church weakened, new ideas – including new religious ones – challenged the hegemony of the Church in Rome. The power of the Church was under attack from all directions, and brewers were often in the vanguard.

the Reformation

The dissolution of the monasteries in England by Henry VIII and his chancellor Thomas Wolsey, with later and similar acts in mainland Europe, effectively signalled the end of the monastic brewing industry. But the seeds of its downfall had been sown earlier. The Church had become a rich and powerful prop of feudalism, out of touch with the spirit of the age and a fetter to the development of a more liberal society. The Abbey of St. Gall in Switzerland, which had started life as a hermit's cell, had become so rich and powerful that the abbots were appointed princes of the Holy Roman Empire. Traders and drinkers railed against a church that insisted on controlling and restricting the sale of beer.

persistent few

The smashing of the monastic way of life in England, cruel and merciless though it was, not only broke the power of the Roman Church but gave great impetus to changes in society that were eventually to bury feudalism and the old social order. Similar changes in mainland Europe – the struggle between Martin Luther and the Catholic hierarchy in Germany, the French Revolution that drove monks from their monasteries, and the Congress of Vienna that placed the Church under the control of the throne and later the state – had an equally profound impact on the power of the church and its role in brewing. Commercial brewing was in the ascendancy. But the monastic way of life continued in a much-diminished form. A handful of monasteries still brew beer today. Inspired by their dedication, other modern brewers help keep that tradition alive, not only in Europe but in North America as well.

1

the beers

Across Europe and North America, breweries large and small continue to craft rich, flavoursome beers in the tradition of the great monastic brewers. Many of these beers are made by monks themselves, working from the seclusion of their abbeys in Belgium and Bavaria. Other monastery-style beers are produced by modern breweries seeking to preserve and emulate the time-honoured traditions and flavours of the medieval monastic brewers.

This chapter provides a country-by-country account of the fascinating and often turbulent histories of these breweries, complete with extensive and tantalizing taster's notes for the beers they produce. The reader also will find special features giving advice on which beers to drink for different seasons and on special occasions.

Belgium

More than any other country, Belgium has drawn world-wide attention to the history and heritage of monastic brewing. The key reason is the presence of the great Trappist breweries, producing some of the best beers in the world.

It can seem strange, even paradoxical, that the Trappist monks, with their famous, if misunderstood, vow of silence, are able to brew and market beer commercially. Although they are not quite so cut off from the world as is often imagined, the Trappist breweries do seem far removed from the hard and ruthless world of commercial brewing, where profits and market share are the only recognised gods.

THE TRAPPIST ORDER

In the 12th century, new ideas of stricter monastic observance were promoted and developed by St. Bernard of Clairvaux, whose monastic order became known as the Cistercians. By the end of the 13th century, the new order had almost 500 monasteries throughout Europe. Gradually, however, the rigour and austerity of the Cistercians began to weaken. The monks of the abbey of La Trappe, founded in Normandy in 1664, were Cistercians who argued for even stricter observance of monastic rules. They became known as the Cistercian Order of the Strict Observance, and are known today as 'Trappists'.

During the French Revolution, in the late 18th century, the Trappists were driven from their monasteries and took refuge in the Low Countries, where they founded new abbeys and brewed beer to sustain their austere lifestyle. Today there are 100 Trappist monasteries and 69 convents, half of them in Europe, although few brew beer commercially.

The Trappists became famous as the 'silent monks'. But although they do prefer an atmosphere of silence, the monks are by no means forbidden to speak, and can exchange views, and discuss ideas and work. Their lifestyle is rugged in the extreme. They have a simple vegetarian diet of bread, cheese and vegetables they make or grow themselves. Although the rules have been softened, at one time Trappists were vegans, avoiding milk and cheese: this made the consumption of vitamin-rich beer all the more essential.

SURVIVAL IN MODERN TIMES

The calm and cloistered buildings of these breathtakingly lovely abbeys are first and foremost places of worship and retreat. The monks brewed originally for themselves, sometimes selling small amounts commercially to help renovate buildings and establish new communities. The development of commercial sales after the Second World War was on a 'survive or die' basis. The monks' breweries had been stripped of copper and other metals by the invading Nazi forces and many of the abbeys had been damaged or destroyed. Income was desperately needed and the monks were forced to sell the beer they so lovingly brewed.

PROTECTING THE TRADITION

Brewing remains unique to each abbey: the monks are at pains to stress there is no such thing as a 'Trappist style' of beer. The only similarity is that their beers are all warm-fermented, members of the ale family, but each house style has evolved in a different way.

Despite these differences the breweries met in 1997 to discuss the formation of the International Trappist Association. They were forced to act as a result of the confusion caused by the growing number of 'abbey' beers – commercial beers that claimed a link to a church or monastery, but had no genuine Trappist connections (see box, page 38). The association places a common seal, 'Authentic Trappist Product', on their beers. This is not an indication of a common style but a guarantee of origin, similar to the appellation system upheld by the wine-growing regions of France.

Vintage beers

The monks, rightly, treat their beers as seriously as wine producers treat their wines. On my first visit, the head brewer, Father Thomas, led me to a sampling room where we tasted several vintages. He expounded on the need to allow the *Grand Cru* versions – sold in Bordeaux-shaped bottles with corks and wire cradles – to breathe when opened, in order to vent off some of the natural carbon dioxide produced during bottle fermentation. All three beers can be laid down to improve, but Father Thomas (who died in 2000) claimed that after five years the two darker ones would develop a 'port wine' character.

chimay

In 1850, 17 Trappist monks at the abbey at Westvleteren were given permission by their abbot to leave the community and build a new abbey on forest land donated by the Prince of Chimay. The Abbaye de Notre-Dame de Scourmont was built ten miles from the village of Forges-les-Chimay in the Ardennes – after which the Chimay brewery is named.

Building work was completed in 1864, but a small brewery had been constructed two years earlier to provide sustenance for the monks and raise funds. Abbey and brewery were built on the site of a well that provided copious amounts of pure water. This water, still drawn from the abbey well, is soft and remarkably free from agricultural and urban impurities.

THE FIRST COMMERCIAL ENTERPRISE

The beer was first made available in bottled form in 1885, and in 1925 the prior allowed wider commercial distribution. It was the first time that Trappist brewers had sold beer to the outside world. During the Second World War, the abbey and brewery were occupied by German forces and vital brewing equipment was removed for the Nazi war effort. When the war ended, the monks needed to sell their beers even more vigorously to help pay for essential rebuilding work.

TASTING NOTES

■ Red or Première (7% abv)

Copper colour with blackcurrant fruit on the aroma and palate, with nutmeg spice and tart hops. The finish is vinous, spicy but with an underlying hop bitterness. Made with pale Pilsner malt, caramalt, German Hallertauer and American Galena hops.

■ White or Cinq Cents (8% abv)

Made with the same hops and malts as Red, this orange-peach coloured beer has a big citrus fruit aroma and palate, a hint of spice in the mouth, and a big, dry finish balanced between tart fruit and bitter hops.

■ Blue or Grande Réserve (9% abv)

A deep copper colour, with an enormous vinous fruitiness on the aroma and palate giving a blackcurrant taste. There is a spiciness from hops and the house yeast, and the big rich and fruity finish becomes dry with a good underpinning of spicy hops. Made with pale Pilsner malt. German Hallertauer and American Galena hops.

PERFECTING THE BREW

The renowned brewing scientist Jean De Clerck from Leuven University's faculty of brewing was called in by Chimay's head brewer. De Clerck advised on the design of new brewing vessels and, crucially, took the house yeast and isolated a pure culture that developed the fruity character of their beers, with their powerful blackcurrant note. When De Clerck died, he was buried in the grounds at Chimay, a rare honour for someone from the secular world.

The Chimay beers are known by the colours of their caps: red, white and blue, and all three are also available in Grand Cru bottles (see box, left). The beers should be served at room temperature, not chilled.

CONTACT

Abbaye de Notre-Dame de Scourmont • rue de la Trappe 294 • B-6464 Forges-les-Chimay • Hainaut
Tel 060-21 0511 • www.chimay.be

ORVAL

Standing in densely wooded countryside, the abbey of Orval has played an important role in the political and spiritual life of the region for centuries. But the present-day beauty and tranquillity of the abbey, and the valley in the

Ardennes in which it stands, mask a turbulent history. Originally founded in 1071 by Benedictine monks from Calabria, Italy, Orval was rebuilt in the 12th century by Cistercians from the Champagne region of France. In 1793 it was sacked following an artillery barrage by French revolutionaries who came over the border into Belgium in the mistaken belief that the deposed Louis XVI was hiding there.

THE ABBEY TODAY

The abbey lay in ruins until the 20th century, when Trappist monks from as far away as Brazil answered a call to rebuild the monastery. The present buildings, constructed over a long period between 1926 and 1948, were designed by the architect Henri Vaes, a great admirer of Cistercian buildings. His impressive creation, with the main abbey buildings reflected in an ornamental lake, is a stunning blend of Romanesque and Burgundian styles, with some startling 1920s Art-Deco touches. Vaes even designed the brewery's pre-Raphaelite beer goblet and the distinctive skittle-shaped bottle used for the beer today.

BREWING AT THE ABBEY

The modern brewhouse was added in 1931. It is in a chapel-like room with a crucifix on the wall, a symbol found in all the Trappist breweries. The formula for the beer sold today

The legend of the valley

The symbol of Orval – a trout with a ring in its mouth – refers to the legend of how the abbey's name was born. In 1076, Countess Matilda of Tuscany came to the valley to visit monks who had come there from Italy. The Countess was in mourning for her late husband. As she sat by the side of a small lake, her wedding ring slipped from her finger into the water. Overcome with grief, she prayed that the ring would be restored to her. At that moment a trout broke the surface of the water with the ring in its mouth. 'This is truly a golden valley!' the Countess exclaimed, and she gave a generous endowment to the monks, who used it to extend the size of the abbey. The name Orval is a reworking of 'Val d'Or' or Golden Valley.

was devised in the 1930s by a German brewer named Pappenheimer, who worked to the monks' specification that includes the English method of 'dry hopping'. This entails adding a handful of hops to the finished beer for aroma and bitterness.

ONE SPECIAL BEER

The brewery is unique among the Trappist establishments in producing just one beer, called simply Orval. Painstaking care and dedication go into every stage of production, starting with the selection of four or five spring barleys from England, France, Germany and the Netherlands. A small amount of English crystal malt is added to the pale varieties to give the beer its distinctive orange-peach colour. The hops used for the boil are German Hallertauer varieties and Styrian Goldings from Slovenia. East Kent Goldings, chosen for their piney and resin aromas, are used for dry hopping. Brewing liquor is still drawn from the well that gave rise to the legend of Orval (see box, left).

Orval has three fermentations. In one of these a wild yeast is used, a member of the same family used in making the 'spontaneous fermentation' lambic beers in the Brussels area. The final fermentation takes place in the bottle: it is stored for six weeks before being released for sale. The acidity of the beer, especially when it is aged for months or a few years, makes it the perfect aperitif.

TASTING NOTES

■ Orval (6.2% abv)

An orange-peach-coloured beer with an aroma of peppery hops and tart fruit. The palate is dominated by gooseberry fruit, with a long and intensely bitter finish with hints of herbs and a touch of lactic sourness from the action of the wild yeast.

CONTACT

Abbaye de Notre-Dame d'Orval • B-6823 Villers-devant-Orval • Tel 06-131 1060 • www.orval.be.

SUMMER BEERS

A time of warm days and long, light evenings, summer is the season when drinkers turn to beers that will refresh and stimulate.

In summer, pale lagers, aromatic wheat beers and golden ales come into their own as drinkers look for beers to quench their thirsts and cool parched throats. In place of warming alcohol, drinkers are looking for a lightness and crispness to suit the bright, clear weather, and a tartness and acidity to help rejuvenate hot, tired limbs.

ORVAL
Orval, Belgium

This golden-peach-coloured beer can be enjoyed at any time, but its pronounced herbal hop aroma, juicy maltiness and quenching acidity make it the ideal summer beer. The 6.2% abv beer has peppery hops and tart fruit on the aroma, and a palate dominated by gooseberry fruit. The intensely bitter finish has hints of herbs and a slight lactic sourness from the action of wild yeast during fermentation.

TRIPEL
Westmalle, Belgium

Westmalle's 9% abv Tripel is a beer big in character and alcohol. With its enticing orange colour, it has become the benchmark for pale Trappist ales. The summery aroma is dominated by floral Saaz hops and orange citrus fruit, the palate has tangy fruit with spicy hop notes, and the long finish has rich alcohol, resiny hops and a herbal note.

SAISON ST. MEDARD
Bailleux, France

Brewed to commemorate St. Medard's day in June, this 7% abv beer has a wonderfully fruity character that makes it a great summer restorative. Although no actual fruit is used, it has both a rich cherry colour and cherry-like aroma. There's full-bodied malt in the mouth, and a tart and fruity finish. According to legend, good weather on St. Medard's day ensures a fine summer, making this the perfect beer to celebrate the warm weather.

HELLES HEFE-WEISSBIER
Spaten-Franziskaner, Germany

This 5% abv pale wheat beer from the Spaten-Franziskaner brewery in Munich has a quenching tartness typical of the style. It has a hazy-gold colour, a fruity, spicy and peppery aroma with a rich banana and cloves palate, and a spicy, fruity and grainy finish. *Hefe* in the name indicates yeast and that the beer is unfiltered, while *weiss* means white. It was the Bavarian nobility who dubbed wheat beer 'white', in order to distinguish it from the brown beers drunk by the common people.

PILS
Weihenstephan, Germany

The brewery faculty in the university of Weihenstephan is on the site of the former Holy Stephan monastery near Munich. Its beers are world classics and include a reviving wheat beer, but it is the pale gold Pils (5.4% abv) that makes the ideal summer refresher, with a pronounced lemon fruit aroma, followed by bitter hops in the mouth and finish, balanced by tart fruit and slightly toasted malt.

LA FIN DU MONDE
Unibroue, Canada

A brewery in the French-speaking part of Canada, Unibroue is influenced by both Northern France and Belgium in its range of beers. Fin du Monde (9% abv) is a pale gold colour with a powerful aroma of citrus fruit, spicy hops and rich malt, followed by a full-bodied malty palate balanced by spicy hops, and a bitter-sweet finish dominated by hops and quenching fruit.

rochefort

Founded in 1230, the secluded abbey of
St. Rémy lies down a narrow, wooded road a
little way from the small town of Rochefort.
Documents show that a small brewery existed
from around 1595, using barley and hops grown
in the grounds. The abbey was destroyed during
the French Revolution – when scant attention
was paid to the border between France and the
Low Countries. In 1887, the abbey was rebuilt
by Trappists from Achel, and a brewery was
opened two years later.

The present brewhouse dates mainly from
the 1960s. Blessed by the customary crucifix on
the wall and the image of St. Arnold, the
brewhouse has burnished copper vessels set
amid tiled walls, the sunlight pouring through
stained-glass windows and glinting on the
mashing vessels and coppers. To make the point
that there is no uniform Trappist style, the
beers from Rochefort are dark and malty, unlike
the pale and intensely bitter beer from
neighbouring Orval. The monk's of St.Rémy
maintain that the character of the ales was
determined by their original importance as a
nutritious supplement to the monastic diet.

TASTING NOTES

■ Six (7.5% abv)

A reddish-brown coloured beer, with a
fruity and slightly herbal aroma and palate,
and a finish dominated by rich malt with
gentle hop notes. Made with Pilsner and
Munich malt, German Hallertauer hop
varieties and Styrian Goldings hops.

■ Eight (9.2% abv)

A copper-brown-coloured beer, with a rich
fruity aroma and palate reminiscent of
raisins and sultanas, with a big finish
dominated by the dark grain and a yeasty-
bread-like note. Made with the same malts
and hop varieties as Six and Ten.

■ Ten (11.3% abv)

A red-brown-coloured beer, with a vast
aroma and palate of toasted grain, soft,
vinous fruits, nuts and chocolate. The finish
is dominated by warming alcohol, with
more chocolate, ripe fruit and gentle hop
notes. Made with the same malts and hop
varieties as Six and Eight.

CONTACT

Abbaye de Notre-Dame de Saint Rémy • B-5580 Rochefort • Tel 08-422 0140

achel

Cistercian monks first settled in this area of Belgium, near the border with the Netherlands, from the 12th century. But it was not until 1845 that the Trappist abbey was founded, dedicated to St. Benedict. Although the monks had been brewing for centuries, the brewery was wrecked during the First World War, and for many years the monks concentrated on farming.

In 1998 it was decided to restore brewing. Many of the monks were unimpressed by the commercial beers available to them, and felt that brewing would be a good way to raise funds for the abbey. The foundation of the brewery was masterminded by Father Thomas, the former head brewer at Westmalle and one of the most revered figures in Trappist brewing.

THE TRAPPIST BREWPUB

Unlike the other monasteries, where the beers are sold at nearby cafes, Achel has built a café in the main abbey, restoring the traditions of centuries ago – although today's 'pilgrims' are attracted by the beer itself. The abbey promotes itself as the only Trappist brewpub in the world.

TASTING NOTES

■ Achelse Blond 4 (4% abv)

A golden beer made with East Kent Goldings, Hallertauer-Hersbrucker and Czech Saaz hops, and Pilsner malt. The beer has a pungent, spicy hop aroma balanced by clean malt, with quenching malt and floral hops in the mouth, and a long, dry finish dominated by spicy hop notes.

■ Achelse Bruine (5% abv)

Made with the same hop varieties as the Blond, together with Caramalt and Pilsner malt, this is a russet-coloured beer with a toasted malt and peppery hops aroma. A firm, malty palate with pronounced touches of malted loaf is followed by a big finish dominated by dark, roasted grain and spicy hops.

CONTACT

Sint-Benedictus Abdij de Achelse Kluis • B-3930 Hamont-Achel • Tel 01-180 0760
www.achelsekluis.be

westmalle

The Trappist abbey of Westmalle stands in flat, wind-swept countryside close to Antwerp. Given the stormy origins of their settlement, the monks had reason to appreciate the protection afforded by the tall elms and high walls that remain around the abbey today.

During the French Revolution, three Trappist monks escaped from France to Switzerland, planning to go to Amsterdam and from there sail to Canada. But concerns over revolutionaries who were still active both in the Low Countries and in North America led the monks to accept an invitation from the Bishop of Antwerp to establish a religious community in his bishopric. They were joined by other refugee Trappists, and a dozen monks set to work to build an abbey in the hard, unyielding countryside. The mellow stone complex was completed in 1804. A brewery was added in 1836 and for some time supplied only the monks' daily needs.

THE BIRTH OF TRAPPISTENBEER

In 1865, the brewery was extended in order to sell beer commercially and help finance a Trappist community in the Belgian Congo. Sales were restricted to the immediate area and were not sold more widely until the 1920s, being given the appellation *Trappistenbeer* in 1932.

Two years later, Abbot Ooms commissioned a secular architect to design a new, bigger brewhouse. Classic copper vessels are set on tiled floors in a powerful 1930s design with Art-Deco influences. The brew kettle is fired by direct flame, a method that gives a defining toasted malt and toffeeish character to the beers, as some of the malt sugars are caramelized during the boil with hops.

THE WESTMALLE BEERS

The monks introduced the designations *Dubbel* and *Tripel* for their two beers and the terms are now widely used throughout Belgium. They are not so much indications of strength, though a Triple is stronger than a Double, but are taken to mean that a Double is darkish and malty, while the Triple, introduced after the Second World War, is pale, hoppy and fruity. Westmalle Tripel has become a world classic; the benchmark beer for strong, pale and hoppy ales.

TASTING NOTES

■ Dubbel (6% abv)

Brewed with Pilsner and dark malts, and Tettnanger, Saaz and Styrian Goldings hops, this russet-coloured beer has a chocolatey, fruity, spicy aroma and palate. The flavour is complex with hints of guava and other tropical fruits. The finish is dry and malty, with chocolate notes from the dark malt and rich fruit.

■ Tripel (9% abv)

This classic Trappist ale is orange-coloured, with a floral Saaz-inspired aroma and orange citrus fruit, followed by a tangy, fruity palate with big spicy hop notes, and a long, lingering finish with warming alcohol, resiny hops and a tantalising herbal character. Made with Pilsner malt, and Tettnanger, Saaz and Styrian Goldings hops.

CONTACT

Abdij Trappisten van Westmalle • Antwerpsesteenweg 496 • B-2390 Westmalle • Tel 03-312 9200

westvleteren

The abbey of St. Sixtus in Westvleteren, the smallest and most reclusive of the Trappist breweries, was founded in 1831 in flat Flanders countryside near Ypres, overlooking the hop fields centred on Poperinge. A small brewery was added in 1838 solely to provide beer for the monks. The beers were first made available outside the cloisters in the 1920s, when the abbot, Dom Bonaventure De Groote, renovated the brewery in local Flemish artisanal style – although the vessels have since been replaced by modern, stainless steel ones.

A RARE BREW

It was monks from Westvleteren who founded the abbey of Chimay in 1850, now the largest and best known of the Trappist breweries. Despite these close links to Chimay, Westvleteren strictly limits the amount of beer it produces commercially. The abbey's distinctive beers are made available for collection on certain days throughout the year. When a new batch is ready, a message on the brewery's answerphone draws queues of drivers in cars, vans – even on bikes – who wait patiently to buy their maximum allowance of ten cases each. Only one beer is available at a time. If no beers are available to take away, the best place to sample them is at the Café De Vrede, just across the street from the abbey.

TASTING NOTES

■ Green Cap or Blond (5.6% abv)
All the Westvleteren beers are made with pale malt and Northern Brewer hops. But where the other beers use dark candy sugar, this pale, gold-coloured 'Blond' beer uses pale candy sugar. A big herbal, hoppy aroma leads to a firm malty body balanced by tart hops, followed by a hoppy, lightly fruity and finally dry finish.

■ Blue Cap (8.4% abv)
A russet-coloured beer, with a vast aroma of tart, plummy fruit, mouth-filling malt, fruit and hops, and a complex finish of rich malt, tart hops and bitter fruit.

■ Yellow Cap or Abbot (10.6% abv)
A dark brown beer, with a massive attack of vinous fruit, toffee and roasted grain on the nose, chewy malt, dark fruit and hops in the mouth, and a warming alcohol, toasted grain and hops finish.

THE WESTVLETEREN BEERS

The beer bottles carry no labels and are identified by the colours of the caps: green, blue and yellow, though the green is also known as Blond, and the yellow as Abbot. While the brewhouse has changed, brewing practice has not. Only pale malt is used, and the beers achieve their colours as a result of white or dark candy sugar. The beers are not filtered – protein and yeast are allowed to drop out naturally during maturation, and the beer is then reseeded with yeast when bottled. There is also an extremely pale, green cap beer, a recent addition to the range.

What's in a name?

In 1946, the monks of St. Sixtus at Westvleteren agreed to license a secular, commercial brewery, St. Bernardus, to brew beers under the name Sixtus and sell them outside of the cloister. Confusion reigned, especially when other commercial breweries sought to follow the example of St. Bernardus, attempting to claim links – often spurious – between themselves and the Trappist order.

A little time after the licence with St. Bernardus expired in 1992, the monks sought to clarify the situation by requesting an end to any suggestion that the secularly-brewed beers came from the Trappist tradition. This helped set in train events that led to the Trappist abbey breweries marking their beers with the hexagonal seal 'Authentic Trappist Product' – finally making a clear distinction between those beers brewed by the Trappist monks themselves, and those beers that merely claimed to be brewed in a 'Trappist' style.

CONTACT

Abdij Sint Sixtus • Donkerstraat 12 • B-8640 Westvleteren • Tel 05-740 0376

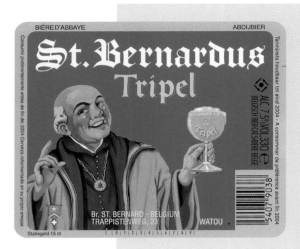

BIÈRE D'ABBAYE   ABDIJBIER

St. Bernardus
Tripel

ALC. 7.5% VOL.33Cl
BELGISCH BIER/ BELGISCHE BIÈRE BELGE

Br. ST. BERNARD - BELGIUM
TRAPPISTENWEG, 23   WATOU

Statiegeld 15 ct

Recommended abbey beers

Abbaye des Rocs 9% abv

Affligem Blond and Dubbel

Augustijn 8% abv and Grand Cru

Corsendonk Pater Noster and Agnus Dei

Dendermonde Tripel

Floreffe Double, Blonde and Triple

Grimbergen Blonde, Tripel and Optimo

Bruno (see page 41)

Leffe Blonde and Brune (see page 39)

Maredsous 6, 8 and 10

St Bernardus Pater 6, Prior 8, Tripel and Abt

What are abbey beers?

Many Belgian breweries now produce beers that they call 'abbey beers'. The term is a very loose one, used to describe beers with some type of connection to a particular monastery or brewed in a style similar to the Trappist abbeys. Unlike the Trappist beers, however, they are not brewed within the abbey itself. In some cases, there are no abbeys at all. Most abbey beers are also filtered and pasteurised, and so do not develop in the bottle.

It was the proliferation of abbey beers in the 1990s that prompted the Trappists to act to protect their name and tradition. Abbey beers, in the view of the Trappists, not only confuse the public but also dilute the importance of the monks' contribution and dedication to good brewing practice. Many of the newer abbey beers, despite the handsome monasteries, stained-glass windows and religious artefacts on their labels, have only the most tenuous links with the religious world. The problem is compounded by the fact that two of the best-known abbey beers, Grimbergen and Leffe (see pages 39–41), are now owned by global brewing conglomerates. Their awesome marketing power means that the beers gain greater attention than the genuine Trappist products, and deepen the confusion.

Nonetheless, some abbey beers do have genuine connections with abbeys that have ceased to brew – in some cases as a result of destruction as long ago as the French Revolution of 1789. In other cases brewing is done under licence from non-brewing abbeys.

Leffe

Belgium's best-known abbey beer, Leffe, is brewed under licence from the Abbaye de Leffe near Namur. The abbey was founded by Norbertine monks in 1152, close to the banks of the River Meuse and its confluence with the smaller River Leff. The community has had a tumultuous history – flooded by the Meuse, ransacked by soldiers during the struggles for control of the Low Countries, destroyed by French revolutionaries, rebuilt, and then bombed during the First World War.

A small brew house is thought to have been built on the site in the 13th century. A new brewery was installed when the abbey was rebuilt in the 18th century, but brewing at the abbey ceased when the community was destroyed during the French Revolution.

LICENSING LEFFE

In the 1950s, with the monks facing severe financial difficulties, a local brewer suggested to the abbot that he should be allowed to produce beers using the Leffe name, and pay the monks a royalty. This arrangement has become the norm for beers with genuine links to abbeys. The Leffe brand is now owned, and assiduously marketed, by the international giant Interbrew.

TASTING NOTES

■ **Leffe Blonde (6.3% abv)**
Brewed with pale malt, and Belgian and German hop varieties. A burnished gold-coloured beer with a fruity and spicy aroma, tart orange fruit and spicy hops in the mouth, and a dry finish balanced between rich malt and hops.

■ **Leffe Brune (6.5% abv)**
A russet-coloured beer with a fruity aroma and hints of dark fruit, a full malty palate with peppery hops, and a finish dominated by dark grain, sultana fruit, hints of chocolate and spicy hops. Made with pale and amber malts, and Belgian and German hop varieties.

CONTACT

Abbaye Notre-Dame de Leffe • Place de l'Abbaye 1 • B-550 Dinant • Tel: 08-222 2377
Interbrew • Vaarstraat 94 • B-3000 Leuven

grimbergen

Founded in Brabant in 1128 by St. Norbert, the Abbaye de Grimbergen has been sacked and pillaged on a regular basis during the conflicts which raged over the Low Countries in the Middle Ages. The abbey has risen phoenix-like from the flames on each occasion – the stunning phoenix symbol that adorns the abbey and the Grimbergen beers is well-deserved.

When the abbey was rebuilt in 1629 – with a Baroque church that still stands today – the monks added a brewery, but it was dismantled during the French Revolution. In 1840, the monks licensed a commercial brewery, Janssens and Peeters, to make beers for them. Inevitably, big business has since stepped in. Since 1958 the brand has been owned by Alken-Maes, and more recently by Britain's biggest brewer, Scottish & Newcastle. Whether the Grimbergen phoenix can survive the onslaught of mammon remains to be seen.

TASTING NOTES

■ Blonde (6.5% abv)

Brewed with pale malt, and Belgian and German hop varieties, this is a burnished gold-coloured beer, with a fruity and hoppy aroma. There is juicy malt and tart fruit in the mouth, and a quenching, fruity finish.

■ Tripel (9% abv)

A bronze-coloured beer with a peppery-spicy hop aroma balanced by rich malt. It has a firm malty body, and a winey-fruity finish balanced by citrus hop flavours. Brewed with pale and caramalt, and Belgian and German hop varieties.

■ Optimo Bruno (10% abv)

This amber-coloured beer is said to be based on an original recipe discovered in the brewery. It has a massive aroma of vinous fruit and alcohol, earthy hops and fat malt in the mouth, and big finish with warming alcohol, vinous fruit and peppery hops. Made with pale and amber malts, and Belgian and German hops.

CONTACT

Abbaye de Grimbergen, Kerkplein 1 • 1850 Grimbergen • Tel: 02-270 9692
Brasserie Union • rue Derbeque 7 • B-6040 Jumet

fRance

It may seem like sacrilege to speak of 'French beer', for this is the world's greatest wine-making country, but Northern France has a long and honourable beer-making tradition that has only recently emerged from the giant shadow cast by wine.

as the Romans marched northwards through Europe, away from the wine-drinking regions to the south, they discovered that the Gauls made potent liquids from grain. By the 9th century, the inhabitants of Northern France were well-respected for these skills: the Emperor Charlemagne even had a Norman brewer brought to his court in Germany.

Today, it is the beers of French Flanders that offer the most quintessentially French style — a rustic farmhouse style known as *bière de garde*.

st. sylvestre

This farmhouse brewery is based in the small Flemish village of the same name, close to the hop-growing area of Hazebrouck. Some claim there has been a brewery there since the 16th century, although the current owners trace the brewery's history to just before the French Revolution of 1789. The address of the brewery, St-Sylvestre-Cappel (Saint Sylvestre's Chapel), reveals the site's religious history – one of the brewery's buildings is a former parish hall.

Historically, these were warm-fermented ales that were brewed in the spring by farmers, using grains and hops from the surrounding fields, and were stored for consumption during the summer months. These bière de garde were seasonal 'keeping beers', brewed in much the same way that they had been in monastic times.

Despite the destruction of the monasteries during the Revolution, the traditional piety of French peasant life means that brewing remains suffused with religious sentiment even today.

TRAPPISTS AND TEMPLARS

It was a a strong 8.5% abv bière de garde called 3 Monts, regarded as one of the finest pale versions of the style, that put St. Sylvestre on the map. Flanders is a notoriously flat landscape and there is a touch of tongue-in-cheek humour to the name of the beer. The 'mountains' referred to are little more than hummocks. One of the hills, Mont des Cats, has a Trappist abbey that used to brew and sell beer in the early part of last century. Although the monks there no longer make beer, the St. Sylvestre brewery commemorates the area's religious roots with an abbey beer called Bière des Templiers. The name is a reference to the Knights Templar, a militant religious order founded during the Crusades, who lived – like the Trappist monks – according to the rule of the Cistercians.

TASTING NOTES

■ Bière des Templiers (8.5% abv)

A russet-coloured beer with a juicy malt and peachy aroma. There is ripe malt in the mouth with a touch of vinous fruit and tart hops, followed by a big finish dominated by rich fruit, creamy malt and gently bitter hops. Brewed with Pilsner and amber malts, together with Flemish Brewers Gold and German Hallertauer hops.

CONTACT

Brasserie de St-Sylvestre • St-Sylvestre-Cappel 59114 Steenvoorde • Tel 03 28 40 15 49 www.brasserie-st-sylvestre.com

castelaín

The Brasserie Castelain, its gleaming coppers visible from the road outside, opened in 1926 in the village of Bénifontaine, north of Lens. The owner, Yves Castelain, calls himself an 'artisan brasseur'. As well as being the first French brewer to produce an organic beer, called Jade, he has been at the forefront of the revival of brewing in the region, proudly claiming to 'preserve the authentic' in French brewing. The brewery's most renowned beer is a classic bière de garde called Ch'ti, but Castelain has also helped restore the monastic tradition, brewing a pale abbey beer called Sint Arnoldus.

"From man's sweat and God's love, beer came into this world."

st. arnold (580-640)

ST. ARNOLD: THE BEER EVANGELIST

According to legend, St. Arnold ended a plague in the city of Metz by plunging his crucifix into a brew kettle and giving the townspeople the blessed beer to drink instead of polluted water. Today, St. Arnold is still celebrated as a patron of brewers, and in the tradition of his monastic forerunners, Castelain keeps a wooden carving of the saint in the brewhouse, to watch over the beer as it brews and bless the brewhouse.

■ **Sint Arnoldus (7.5% abv)**
What the French call 'une blonde', Sint Arnoldus is a pale beer with an enticing aroma of crisp, slightly toasted malt, citrus fruits and spicy hops. There is a firm, malty body balanced by fruit and hops, and a massive finish dominated by spicy hops, tart fruit and ripe, juicy malt. Made with pale malt from Flemish and Gatinais barleys, together with Belgian and German Hallertauer hops, the beer is reseeded with yeast in the bottle and improves with age.

CONTACT

Brasserie Castelain • 13 rue Pasteur • Bénifontaine • 62410 Wingles
Tel 03 21 08 68 68 • www.chti.com.

ᴏuyck

Like many of the region's breweries, Duyck began life as a small farm brewery. Today, the brewery is renowned for a classic bière de garde, Jenlain, but also brews an abbey beer, St. Druon de Sebourg. The church in Sebourg has been a place of pilgrimage since the 12th century, when St. Druon walled himself up in a small cell there. For almost 40 years the hermit survived on a diet of water and barley – an appropriate choice of diet, perhaps, for someone who has lent his name to a beer.

TASTING NOTES

■ St. Druon de Sebourg (6.8% abv)

A golden beer with a rich and tempting aroma of biscuity malt and spicy hops. Sweet malt and hops dominate the palate, with some citrus fruit, while the finish is warming, creamily malty, with good spicy hop notes and a lingering hint of tart fruit.

CONTACT

Brasserie Duyck • 113 rue Nationale • 59144 Jenlain
Tel 03 27 49 70 03 • www.duyck.com

La choulette

The original brewery, known as Bourgeois-Lecerf, was founded in Hordain, in 1885, close to the ruins of the vast 12th-century Cistercian abbey of Vaucelles. In 1977, the brewery was bought by the present owner, Alan Dhaussy, who soon discovered old Bourgeois-Lecerf recipes from pre-lager days and fashioned a group of beers under the La Choulette label, including an amber beer, a framboise with raspberry juice and an abbey beer.

MONKS AND REVOLUTIONARIES

Dhaussy has always made his beers with an eye to brewing history. His name first became widely recognised in 1986, with the launch of La Bière des Sans Culottes. The beer was named after the urban poor of the French Revolution, which did so much to destroy the monasteries in France, allowing commercial brewing to flourish. To prove how even-handed he is, Dhaussy also makes a golden abbey beer, named L'Abbaye de Vaucelles, to mark those great brewing traditions that disappeared as a result of the Revolution.

CONTACT

Brasserie La Choulette • 16 rue des Ecoles • 59111 Hordain
Tel 03 27 35 72 44

TASTING NOTES

■ **L'Abbaye de Vaucelles (7.5% abv)**
A golden beer with a superbly aromatic nose of toasted malt and spicy hops, with malt, hops and citrus fruit on the palate, followed by a finish balanced between warming alcohol, sweet malt, tart fruit and gently bitter hops. Brewed with pale malt from French barley, and Belgian and German Hallertauer hop varieties.

Abbaye de Vaucelles

Bière blonde artisanale

75 cl ℮   7,5% vol.

Bailleux

The Bailleux brewery, tucked away up winding roads in the thickly wooded hills of Hainaut on the Franco-Belge border, produces beer called Saison St. Médard, which first appeared on 8 June 1989 – St. Médard's Day in the French calendar. French brewing traditions are closely bound to the soil and the seasons, and St. Médard, a 6th-century bishop of Noyen, is still venerated in Northern France as a patron of harvests. A local proverb claims that if it rains on St. Médard's Day, it will rain for another 40 days. A suitable figure, then, for the region's rural brewers to commemorate with this classic bière de garde.

■ **Saison St. Médard (7% abv)**

This bière de garde is brewed with pale, amber and dark malts, together with Belgian Brewers' Gold, German Hallertauer, Hersbrucker and Spalter hops, giving a rich cherry colour and a cherry-like aroma and palate (although no fruit is used). There is full-bodied malt in the mouth, and the finish is tart, fruity and dry. The beer is refermented in the bottle. A darker version, with a chocolatey flavour, is produced for the Christmas period.

CONTACT

Brasserie Bailleux • Café-Restaurant au Baron de Gussignies • Place au Fond des Rocs
Gussignies • 59570 Bavay • Tel 03 27 66 88 61

the netherlands

A strong and venerable brewing tradition is still maintained in Holland, a country that separated from its neighbour Belgium – the giant of monastic brewing – only in the 19th century.

To most of the world, Dutch beer is either Heineken, its subsidiary Amstel, or the beers from the independent Grolsch in their charmingly old-fashioned, swing-top bottles. These international brands, based on Pilsner-style lagers, mask the powerful historic roots of Dutch brewing. In fact, both Heineken and Grolsch brew more traditional dark beers, and a smaller Heineken subsidiary makes excellent Bocks. There is also a sturdy independent sector producing beers with a deep bow in the direction of the monastic tradition. One brewery, La Trappe, is actually attached to a Trappist abbey.

La trappe

The abbey of Koningshoeven proclaims its lineage proudly, naming its beers La Trappe in honour of the original Trappist settlement in Normandy. Built in a style best described as 'Gothic Severe', the abbey was the result of the labours of Trappist monks in the 1880s. Expelled from France during the Revolution, these monks travelled further north than their brothers who stayed in Belgium, settling near Tilburg in the Brabant region, which straddles the Belgian-Dutch border. Surrounded and defended by tall trees and a lake, the abbey was built on land donated by the Dutch monarch: Koningshoeven means 'the King's Gardens'.

It was the first abbot, the son of a brewer from Munich, who added the brewery to help finance the construction of the abbey. It has the rustic name of Schaapskooi, which means 'sheep fold', but has the appearance of a railway signal-box. For many years, the abbey produced just one beer called Dubbel, but a Tripel and a Quadrupel joined it, followed, rather oddly, by an Enkel – the lowest-strength beer in the range. This beer had been brewed for some time for the sole consumption of the monks of Koningshoeven, but was put on public sale in 1995 to meet the demand for a paler and weaker member of the range.

THE MONKS AND THE COMMERCIAL WORLD

In common with all the Trappist breweries, Koningshoeven has had its fair share of turbulence. After the Second World War, in their first brush with the commercial world, the monks sold their brewery to the Belgian group Stella Artois, which wanted to develop a greater presence in the Netherlands. It installed a small lager brewing plant and produced a beer with the unlikely name of Trappist Pils. The beer was not a success, Stella Artois retreated back to Belgium, and the monks raised the necessary money to buy back their brewery: it's the only known example of a 'monks' buy-out'. The monks had stored their brewing equipment and, crucially, their yeast, and started to brew again, for their own needs and for commercial sales.

GENUINE TRAPPIST BEERS?

While the beers may be proudly labelled La Trappe, the brewery's Trappist credentials are entangled in controversy. Since 1999 the brewery has been owned by the brewing giant Bavaria, best known for 'label beers' – beers brewed specifically for supermarkets. Bavaria claims Koningshoeven is still a Trappist brewery, and that the monks control the brewing process. As far as the International Trappist Association is concerned, however, only the abbey belongs to the brotherhood, while the beers and brewery have been relegated to the status of abbey beers.

The controversy is likely to continue. La Trappe beers exported to other countries still carry the appellation '*Trappistenbier*', and it may need the intervention of the Vatican to sort out the problem. In the 1990s, Koningshoeven had to seek Papal blessing to produce an own-label Trappist beer for the British supermarket group Sainsbury's. Ultimately, Koningshoeven may pay a high price for its relationship with the commercial world, but at present, whether they are labelled Trappist or Abbey, these are undoubtedly beers of the highest quality.

TASTING NOTES

■ Enkel (5.5% abv)

Originally brewed only for the consumption of the monks, this is a golden beer with a slight amber note, and a burst of rich, floral, citrus hops on the nose. There is a juicy malt and bitter hop palate, and a quenching finish balanced between biscuity malt, bitter hops and tart fruit. Made using pale malt, with a touch of Munich malt, and Hallertauer and Northern Brewer hops.

■ Dubbel (6.5% abv)

The original beer brewed at the abbey, the La Trappe Dubbel is tawny-coloured, with a pronounced aroma and palate similar to Orange Muscat, balanced by peppery hops. There is a big finish with spicy hops, tart fruit and rich malt. Pale, Munich and other coloured malts are used, with Hallertauer and Northern Brewer hops.

■ Tripel (8% abv)

With pale and Munich malts, and Goldings hops, this is a bronze-coloured beer with a massive attack of spicy Goldings on the nose. There are more tart and spicy hops in the mouth balanced by rich orange fruit and juicy malt, followed by a long finish dominated by bitter hops and tart fruit.

■ Quadrupel (10% abv)

This red-bronze beer is brewed as an annual vintage and is launched every autumn. It is deceptively smooth, with a rich orange fruit aroma balanced by spicy hops, a palate dominated by biscuity malt, spices and hops, and a long smooth finish with creamy malt, gentle spices and delicate hops, all underscored by warming alcohol. Brewed using pale and Munich malts, together with Hallertauer and Northern Brewer hops.

The Eleventh Commandment

The Arcen brewery (pronounced with a soft 'C' to the amusement of English-speakers), lies in the town of the same name in the Limburg province. Its speciality is a beer called Het Elfde Gebod, which means 'The Eleventh Commandment'. In the Catholic areas of the Low Countries this is a convivial request to eat and drink well. If only the other ten were as inviting.

Het Elfde Gebod (7% abv) is a golden ale with a powerful fruity aroma of apples and a gentle underpinning of spicy hops, with rich fruit, biscuity malt and tart fruit in the mouth, and a finish that starts sweet and malty but becomes dry and bitter with more rich fruitiness. It is made with pale and amber malts, and Belgian and German hop varieties. A truly heavenly beer.

"There is no beer in heaven
so we drink it here"

*inscription on the wall of the
brew house at la trappe*

CONTACT

Abdij Onze Lieve Vrouw van Koningshoeven/Trappistenbierbrouwerij de Schaapskooi
Eindhovenseweg 3 • NL-5056 RP Berkel-Enschot • Tel: 013-543 6124 • www.latrappe.nl

Brouwhuis maximiliaan

This Amsterdam-based brewpub, built on the site of an old medieval brewery, brews Bock and wheat beers in the tradition of the medieval monastic breweries. The brothers Albert and Casper Hoffman opened their brewpub on the site of the brewery of the monastery of Bethaniën in 1992. The building stands today on the edge of Amsterdam's notorious Red Light district, offering a curious and possibly unique meeting point of brewery and brothels.

Fortunately, the bar and restaurant attract serious beer lovers, rather than those in search of the pleasures of the flesh.

THE BROUWHUIS BREWHOUSE

It took a Dutch firm a-year-and-a-half to build the hand-hammered copper vessels, the result of a world tour of brewpubs by Albert Hoffman. The burnished mashing and boiling kettles are on view in a large drinking area at the back of the pub, with a barrel-vaulted ceiling.

The brewpub concentrates on ales brewed with warm-fermenting yeast. In the style of artisan breweries in French Flanders and Belgium, the mash tun doubles as the copper: the wort is pumped from the vessel to a second one called a lauter tun, where it is clarified, and returned to the mash tun for the boil with hops.

THE MONASTIC TRADITION

While the Hoffmans produce a large and constantly changing range, the regular beers pay homage to the monastic tradition. A beer named Bethaniën, for example, commemorates the medieval monastery brewery on whose site the Hoffmans brew today. But it is the seasonal Bock beers and wheat beers, such as Bethaniën's Maximator, which imitate the styles of Bavaria's monastic breweries and owe most to the monastic traditions.

TASTING NOTES

■ **Bethaniën (4.5% abv)**

Made with 100 per cent pale malt, and Saaz and Perler hops, this pale gold beer gives a delightful waft of perfumy and floral hops, followed by succulent malt and tart hops in the mouth, a long finish with sweet malt, gently bitter hops, and hints of tart citrus fruit.

■ **Meibock (6.5% abv)**

This golden-amber-coloured Bock beer is brewed with caramalt, pale malt and Saaz hops. There is a sweet malt aroma with a touch of nuts, a good balance of delicate hops and rich malt in the mouth, and a lingering bitter-sweet finish with a touch of lemon fruit and creamy malt. Brewed for the spring season.

■ **Maximator Wheatbock (6.5% abv)**

Brewed with a Bavarian yeast strain, wheat and barley malt and Saaz hops, this cloudy amber beer has a typical South German aroma of banana and cloves, with a bready-yeasty palate and more fruit and spices that linger on into the finish. Wonderfully refreshing.

■ **Caspers Max Tripel (7.5% abv)**

A pale russet beer with a massive aroma of spicy hops and vinous fruit. Spices, rich malt and hops dominate the palate, while the finish has a superb balance of ripe malt, spicy hops and vinous fruit. Made with pale and amber malt and Saaz hops.

CONTACT

Brouwhuis Maximiliaan • Kloveniersburgwal 6–8 • 1012 CT Amsterdam
Tel: 020-626 6280 • www.maximiliaan.nl

BRAND

Dating from 1341, Brand is the oldest brewery in the Netherlands. The Brand family took over ownership of the medieval brewery in 1871, when the previous owner sold his brewery in disgust after failing to prevent the road to his brewery cafe from being redirected towards the town's church. The family kept control of the brewery until it was bought by Heineken in 1990. Cynics expected its imminent closure, but Brand has continued with a considerable amount of independence: its survival may be not unconnected to the fact that in 1971 the brewery's beers were awarded the Royal seal.

DUTCH BOKS

The Dutch have adopted and then adapted the German Bock style, making it a beer of their own and usually changing the spelling to *Bok*. Most Dutch Boks are warm-fermenting members of the ale rather than the lager family, which means they are not true descendants of the German style. Brand's Bocks are a notable exception, being brewed by cold-fermentation in the style of Bavaria's monastic breweries.

TASTING NOTES

■ Imperator (6.5% abv)

Inspired by the great Munich Bocks such as Salvator, Imperator has an amber-gold colour, a big sappy aroma of rich malt and hops, a firm malty body balanced by perfumy hops and a dry finish with a fine balance of malt and bitter hops.

■ Meibock (7% abv)

A golden beer in the style of a Munich spring Maibock, it has a pronounced spicy and citrus aroma, with citrus fruit dominating the palate and a long, finish with malt, tart fruit and bitter hops.

■ Dubbelbock (7.5% abv)

A winter special with a glowing port-wine colour, a deep aroma of fruit, floral hops and chocolate, creamy malt and dark fruit dominating the palate and a big fruit, chocolate and hop finish.

CONTACT

Koninklijke Brand Bierbrouwerij BV • Brouwerijstraat 2 • Postbus 1 • 6300 AA Wijlre
Tel: 044-508282 • www.heineken.com

EASTER BEERS

Easter is a time of change and renewal for monks and pagans alike: while drinkers shake off the winter chill with rich, warming beers, brewers herald the arrival of warm weather with lighter, crisper brews.

Traditionally, Easter marks the end of Lent, when Christians commemorate Christ's sojourn in the wilderness by fasting for 40 days and nights. During Lent, monks brewed strong, full-bodied beers to drink. This 'liquid bread' provided essential nourishment throughout the period of fasting and denial. This tradition continues today, and one of the best-known of these Lenten beers is Paulaner's Salvator, a rich Doppelbock best saved for the cooler, still-chilly weather before Easter.

With the arrival of warmer weather after Easter, the time comes for drinking lighter, more refreshing beers. Warm weather once signalled the end of the brewing season, since beer risked being spoiled in the heat, and spring was the last opportunity to taste the freshly brewed beers before they were laid down to keep in cool cellars. Today, drinkers still welcome in the spring season with light, refreshing beers such as clean, hoppy Maibocks and pale Helles Bocks.

SALVATOR DOPPELBOCK
Paulaner, Germany

Named *Salvator* – Saviour – in honour of Christ, this rich 7.5% abv beer is the benchmark for Bavarian Bocks. It is lagered for three months and then ceremonially tapped three or four weeks before Easter in the brewery beer garden. This welcomes in the *starkbierzeit*, or strong-beer period,

when drinkers invade Munich's beer gardens to sup Salvator and other rich brews that help shake off the memories of the long alpine winter. Drinking Doppelbock is known as the *frühlingskur* – the spring cure. Salvator is a russet-coloured beer with a rich malt-loaf aroma, a yeasty-bready palate, and a complex finish with sultana-like fruit, malt and hops.

MAIFEST
Sudwerk, USA

An American brewery with powerful German roots, Sudwerk's 6.5% abv Maifest is – in the tradition of the Bavarian Maibocks – lighter and hoppier than traditional Bocks, making it an excellent spring refresher in warm weather. It has a copper colour, with a malty and spicy hops aroma, nuts and malt in the mouth, and a big finish with creamy malt and tart, bitter hops.

HELLES BOCK
Andechs, Germany

A 6.8% abv pale Bock beer brewed in the beautiful monastery of Andechs. Pale amber in colour with a rich sweet malt aroma and hints of citrus fruit and delicate floral hops, this is a fresh, vernal beer, well-suited to spring-time drinking. Rich malt dominates the palate while the finish is lingering, balanced between malt, hops and tart fruit.

EASTER SPECIAL SPINGO
Blue Anchor, England

The powerful beers brewed at the Blue Anchor, the site of a medieval monks' hospice, hark back to a time when ales were rich, strong and seasonal, the perfect warmers on a cool spring evening. The 7.6% abv Easter Special is a dark ruby colour with earthy blackcurrant fruit balanced by spicy hops on the aroma, dry fruit and malt in the mouth, and a finish that is long, fruity and yeasty, with hints of vanilla, caramel and peppery hops.

ST. GALLER LANDBIER
Schützengarten, Switzerland

Brewed in the city founded by St. Gall, the patron saint of Swiss brewers, Landbier is a cloudy yellow wheat beer, quenching but flavourful. There are ripe aromas of banana and cloves, a palate dominated by fruit and spices, and a lingering finish with fruit, spices and gentle hops.

KING CNUT ALE
St. Peter's, England

Because it uses nettles in place of hops, King Cnut's Ale (5% abv) can only be brewed in the spring when a supply of fresh nettles become available. Nettles come from the same plant family as hops, and were widely used, together with a host of other plants, spices and herbs, before the hop became universal. The beer is a reminder of the days when brewing was a seasonal industry, and spring beers used the plants that burst forth after the long winter. King Cnut Ale, dark russet in colour, has a smoky, nutty, roasted grain aroma, and a powerful waft of juniper. The palate is tart and spicy with a hint of rhubarb fruit. The finish is dry, bitter, spicy, fruity and peppery.

germany

The monastic brewing tradition flourishes in Germany, especially in the vast southern region of Bavaria. The Bavarians have kept alive traditions lost to the Protestant North, brewing powerful beers known as Bock.

Bavaria is the biggest beer-drinking region in the world. Germany as a nation has 1,400 breweries, and 750 of them are based in Bavaria. Away from the powerhouse of Munich and its giant producers, many of the breweries are small, serving villages and small towns. In these rural areas, small-scale monastic brewing continues in a few abbeys, much as it has done for centuries. Several larger breweries with long and venerable monastic roots, survive in Munich – the first city to embrace the lagering system of beer production. Paulaner, Spaten-Franziskaner and, just north of the city, Weihenstephan, are all now sizeable commercial breweries – but they still help to keep alive the traditions of monastic brewing, including Bock and wheat beers.

THE MONKS' PLACE

The German for Munich is *München*, a corruption of *Mönchen*, which means 'the Monks' Place'. Celtic tribes settled in the Munich area at the foothills of the Alps between 500 and 15 BC, but it was Benedictine monks who first developed a distinct settlement there in the 8th century. Later, communities of Augustinians and Franciscans, among others, also built monasteries there and set up breweries to help nourish and refresh them. The importance of the monks was enshrined in the name Mönchen, given to the settlement in 1158 by Duke Henry the Lion.

The term 'liquid bread' comes from Munich and signifies the importance given to the strong beers of Lent that sustained the monks during their period of fasting. The Munich brewers even adopted their own patron saint, St. Benno. One of Munich's oldest breweries, Löwenbräu (Lion Brew), used to make a strong beer called St. Benno for the Lent period.

THE BIRTH OF BOCK BEERS

Although not themselves monastic, the breweries of the town of Einbeck were instrumental in the creation of the 'Bock' style of beer – a style which the Bavarian monastic breweries were to later adopt.

The citizens of Einbeck were granted brewing rights in the 14th century. They spread malt and hops in the lofts of their houses to dry, while a communal brewing vessel toured the city for them to use in turn. The specially high arches of the houses, designed to allow the vessel to pass through, are still visible today.

The origins of Bock-style beer lie in Einbeck, stressed by the legend above the Einbecker Brewery: '*Ohne Einbeck gäb's kein Bockbier*' – 'Without Einbeck there would be no Bock beer'. To emphasize the point, all the brewery's products are labelled *Ur-Bock*, meaning Original Bock, while the entrance to Einbeck has a sign saying 'Beer City'.

FROM BECK TO BOCK

The people of Munich and Bavaria first came across Einbecker beer in the 17th century when the Duke of Brunswick in Lower Saxony married the daughter of a Bavarian aristocrat. The wedding was held in Munich and the duke brought a master brewer with him to make beer for the celebration. The Bavarians took to the strong, rich style and, over the course of time, their powerful southern dialect turned Einbecker into '*Oanbocker*'. By the 18th century, the Munich Hofbräuhaus (the Royal Court Brewery) was producing an Oanbock beer. This in turn was shortened to the simple and explosive 'Bock'. The new name was a pun. Bock in the Bavarian dialect means billy-goat and, as a symbol of virility and strength, was the ideal name for the beer style. Adopted by many of the monastery breweries of Munich as

beer. The decision was not entirely altruistic – the Bavarian royal family held a monopoly over the growing of barley. Hops were added to the mix when they began to be used widely in brewing. Today, the law remains in force across Germany, and is viewed as an icon of the nation's proud brewing traditions.

The Reinheitsgebot did at first restrict the range of ingredients that the monastic brewers could use in their beer – and may well have prevented the development of the diverse monastic styles that can be now found in Belgium. Many foreign brewers argue that the Reinheitsgebot places too many restrictions on brewing skills, and that the adroit use of other cereals and specialist sugars can improve the enjoyment of beer. On the other hand, the law does mean that American-style lagers, made with large amounts of rice or corn, cannot be foisted on German drinkers. It is because of the Reinheitsgebot that modern German beers retain a traditional style and flavour missing from most international lager brands.

MODERN STYLES

The beers brewed for centuries by the monks would have been either wheat beers or brown beers made from barley malt. The strong Bock beers brewed by monastic and commercial breweries in Bavaria today were not adopted until the 18th century and now use the lager or cold storage method – although some strong

their own, the Bock style of beer – strong, lagered for several months, and often dark – is today most closely linked to Bavaria.

THE PURITY LAW

The Bavarian *Reinheitsgebot*, or Purity Law, has been a major influence on monastic brewing in Germany. Introduced in 1516 by the dukes of Bavaria, the law laid down that only malted barley, yeast and water could be used to make wheat beers, called '*Weissbock*', are still produced by an older method similar to ale-brewing. One reason that Munich's monastic breweries are so successful today is that they encouraged and embraced the innovations that occured in the city. It was in ice-filled caves in the foothills of the Alps that Munich brewers made the first tentative attempts to ferment and mature beers at low temperatures to keep them free from infection in the summer months – thereby discovering the lagering process. And it was in Munich in the 19th century that Gabriel Sedlmayr the Younger, using the new technologies of the Industrial Revolution, made lager-brewing a commercial reality at his Spaten Brewery. Munich's role as one of the great brewing centres was aided by the development of hop-growing in the Hallertau region to the north, now the world's largest hop-growing area.

Martin Luther

The beers of Einbeck have an intriguing link to the man who did more than any other to destroy the power of the Catholic Church. Supplies of Einbeck beer were sent to Martin Luther to sustain him during the Lenten fast which preceded his appearance at the Diet of Worms in 1521. Luther, an Augustinian friar, was outlawed in the presence of the emperor Charles V, but the disobedient monk had cause to thank the brewers of Einbeck for their nourishing beer at his trial. Luther's opposition to the Church of Rome made him a national hero and set the stage for the Protestant Reformation.

In 1525, when Luther married a former nun, Katherine of Bora, the couple were once again given a cask of the town's Einbeck beer. Ironically, the Bock style of beer, so closely associated with Martin Luther, now survives and flourishes in the one part of Germany where his reformation failed to take root – the Catholic heartlands of Bavaria.

paulaner

The Paulaner brewery was founded sometime before 1634 by the followers of St. Francis of Paula, a Franciscan friar from Italy. The monks built their monastery on a hill on the outskirts of Munich and added a small brewery. The hillside was chosen as it would help the monks defend themselves: it later proved invaluable when maturation cellars needed to be dug so that beers from the brewery could be lagered.

The monks made, among others, a strong beer for the Lent period called Salvator, which means Saviour. When the term Bock was applied to strong beers, Salvator and its rivals were dubbed *Doppelbock*, because of their exceptional strength. Salvator is the classic Munich Bock and the benchmark for the style.

SALVATOR

In the late 19th century, when the monastery was secularised, the new owner vigorously promoted sales of Salvator, with such success that other Munich brewers launched their own brands under the same name. Paulaner took them to court in 1894, with the result that its competitors dropped the name but gave their brands new titles ending in '-or'. Today there are such brands as Augustiner's Maximator, Löwenbräu's Triumphator and Spaten's Optimator. So famous is Paulaner's Bock that the word 'Salvator' has been incorporated into the company name. The brewery's full title – Paulaner-Salvator-Thomasbräu – also includes the name of a long-extinct brewery, founded by monks in honour of the Apostle Thomas, which was taken over along the way.

TASTING NOTES

■ **Paulaner Salvator Doppelbock (7.5% abv)**

This very strong, russet-brown-coloured beer is brewed with pale lager malt, caramalt, Munich malt and Hallertauer variety hops. There is a rich malt loaf aroma, a yeasty, bready palate, and a complex finish rich in sultana-like fruit, malt and hops. The beer is lagered (stored) for at least three months.

CONTACT

Paulaner-Salvator-Thomasbräu • Hochstrasse 75 • 81541 Munich
Tel: 089-480050 • www.paulaner.de

weihenstephan

The monastery at Weihenstephan was founded in 724, when an Irish Benedictine monk named Korbinian established a community there. He called it Sacred Stephen in honour of the first Christian martyr, which became Weihenstephan in German. The monastery was built on a hill (useful later when lagering cellars were needed) on the outskirts of Freising, close to Munich.

EARLY BREWING

Hops were grown in the area around the abbey as early as 768. The monks were certainly brewing beer by 1040, when they were granted the right to sell their beer to aid their work in the community, but they were probably making beer for themselves at a much earlier date. With some justification, its beer labels claim the brewery to be the '*Ältester brauerei der Welt*' – the 'oldest brewery in the world'.

Over the centuries, the monastery and brewery have been attacked, sacked and rebuilt. Although the Church was secularised after the Congress of Vienna in 1815, the site still has the genuine feel of monastic cloisters. The modern brewery, which retains a chapel-like atmosphere with high, vaulted windows, produces 200,000 hectolitres a year, nearly three-quarters of which is devoted to wheat beer.

THE UNIVERSITY

Courses in brewing techniques started at Weihenstephan before the First World War. The ancient abbey is now a fully fledged university run by the Ministry of Culture and the world's most revered faculty of brewing.

TASTING NOTES

■ Original (5.4% abv)

Pale lager malt gives the beer a pale-golden colour, and the Hallertauer hop varieties lend an aromatic floral and slightly spicy hop nose. This is followed by a quenching juicy malt palate balanced by tart hops. A tart and refreshing hint of lemon fruit dominates the malty, hoppy finish.

■ Pils (5.4% abv)

Made with the same malt and hops as the Original, this is a golden beer with a pronounced lemon-citrus fruit aroma. Intensely bitter and hoppy in the mouth and finish, the bitterness is balanced by rich, toasted malt.

■ Hefeweissbier Dunkel (5.3% abv)

Hefe means yeast and weissbier is wheat beer. This beer is made with pale and dark wheat and barley malts, as well as Hallertauer hops. An amber-red beer with a dense creamy head, the aroma has a pronounced banana note, with hints of roasted grain and chocolate. The dense palate is dominated by rich grain and fruit, and followed by a long finish finely balanced between grain and fruit, with a delicate touch of hops.

■ Hefeweissbier (5.4% abv)

The blend of pale malt wheat and malted barley give this wheat beer a much lighter, hazy amber colour than the Dunkel version. The Hallertauer hops give the beer a big peppery, spicy aroma, with banana and vanilla in the mouth, and a long creamy malt finish balanced by light hop notes.

CONTACT

Bayerische Staatsbrauerei Weihenstephan • Postfach 1155 • Freising • Munich
Tel: 08161-13004 • www.brauerei-weihenstephan.de

andechs

The 15th-century abbey of Andechs lies in the foothills of the Bavarian Alps, between Augsburg and Munich. The site was originally dominated by a castle belonging to the counts of Diessen, and has been a place of pilgrimage ever since the relics of St. Rasso were transferred to the castle for safe-keeping in AD 955. In the 12th century, three Sacred Hosts (wafers) – two of which were consecrated by Pope Gregory I, the other by Pope Leo IX – were added to the castle's relics. The beautiful Baroque monastery remains a place of veneration, although today's pilgrims are more likely to be attracted by Andechs' beers and the renowned beer garden.

THE CLOISTER BREWERY

In 1455, Duke Albert III handed over the castle's collegiate church to Benedictine monks. Their monastery became an abbey three years later. The abbey was secularised in 1803, restored in 1850, and has been brewing fine Bock beers ever since. Today, Andechs is among a handful of German monasteries where brewing continues to be practised by the monks themselves. The chapel crypt has a superb 18th-century design in Rococo style: the crypt has the remains of Carl Orff, composer of the *Carmina Burana*, which takes its lyrics directly from an old Benedictine manuscript.

A PROFITABLE BUSINESS

Magnificent copper kettles supply a vast beer hall and a garden that offers fine views of the surrounding countryside. Brewing is now the monastery's major source of income. The monks have even licensed a Canadian company, – Brick Brewing – to produce their beers in North America. St. Benedict, the father of European monasticism, enjoined his monks to work to support themselves: the monks of Andechs have certainly taken his rule to heart.

FESTIVAL BEERS

For centuries, seasonal festivals and holidays have been celebrated with drinking and feasting. Beer, often especially brewed for the occasion, has long been an important accompaniment to the revels.

Important religious holidays such as Christmas and Easter were not only times for prayer and thanksgiving, but also for drinking and celebration. The traditional season for beer festivals, however, is early autumn, when festivals were held to mark the start of the new brewing season, to finish off the last of the beer stored during the summer and to taste the first batch of the new season's beer. The tradition continues today with the great Munich Oktoberfest (see box, right), and the strong, full-bodied Märzen and Oktoberfest beers drunk during these celebrations are modern descendants of earlier seasonal, festive beers.

But beer festivals can be staged at any time of the year, and many modern festivals offer a far greater choice of beer than the Oktoberfest. The Great American and Great British Beer Festivals offer well over a thousand different beers – the perfect opportunity to sample a wide range of different styles.

OKTOBERFESTBIER
Spaten, Germany

Spaten's beer is, by tradition, the first to be tapped at the Munich Oktoberfest. The 5.9% abv beer is gold-coloured, with a firm malty aroma and body balanced by floral hops and a hint of lemon citrus fruit. It is wonderfully quenching, a fine example of a strong Munich lager, but some way removed from the reddish March beers that used to be brewed and stored for the beer festival.

MÄRZEN
Sudwerk, USA

Before refrigeration, when warm weather risked spoiling the brew, beers were made in March, and stored in deep cellars to last through the summer. When the cooler autumn weather arrived and brewing could begin once again, great festivals were held to finish the last remaining stocks of the March (Märzen) beers. Today's rich, bottom-fermenting Märzens, a 19th-century development of this festive style, are still brewed in the spring, stored during the summer and often tapped in autumn festivals. Sudwerk's 5.2% abv version, which takes its amber colour from the use of darker malt, has a rich malt and tangy hops aroma and palate, and a big finish with juicy malt and spicy hops.

ABBOT ALE
Greene King, England

Greene King's 5% abv Abbot Ale not only celebrates the monastic traditions of Bury St Edmunds but is a classic example of a premium English ale. It has a fine copper-red colour, tart hops and ripe fruit on the aroma, nutty malt and fruit in the mouth, and an intense, bitter-sweet finish.

OKTOBERFEST
Penn Brewing, USA

This North American brewery produces an excellent version of the festival beer style with its 5.6% abv Oktoberfest. It has an amber colour, with juicy malt balanced by tangy hops on the aroma, a malty and nutty palate, and a dry finish with a good spicy hop note that balances biscuity malt. The brewery holds its own local version of the Oktoberfest every year during the last two weekends of September.

L'ABBAYE DE VAUCELLES
La Choulette, France

As well as commemorating the monastic tradition, La Choulette's 7.5% abv abbey beer is a magnificent example of a strong bière de garde. This classic seasonal French beer style was brewed in spring to be drunk during the warm weather, and the remnants were consumed in the autumn festivities. It is a golden beer with an aromatic nose of toasted malt and spicy hops, with malt, hops and citrus fruit on the palate, and warming alcohol, sweet malt, tart fruit and bitter hops in the finish.

THE MUNICH OKTOBERFEST

The modern celebrations were first held in 1810 to celebrate the wedding of Prince Ludwig of Bavaria, but the roots of the festival go back further, to medieval festivities held to mark the start of autumn. The 16-day festival, which lasts until the first Sunday of October, has since developed into a gigantic beer drinking event attracting millions of visitors from across the world to the tents of local Munich brewers.

ASAM DOPPELBOCK
Weltenburg, Germany

This 6.5% abv beer is a magnificent example of the strong Bock beers that refreshed monks and eased their hard life and grinding poverty. A classic German Bock, this is a beer that would grace any festival. The beer has a cappuccino head and a ruby-black colour, with a malty and liquorice aroma. There are dark malt, bitter chocolate and floral hops in the mouth, and a big finish dominated by toasted, smoky malt.

■ **Helles Bock (6.8% abv)**
Made with pale lager malt and Hallertauer hop varieties, this pale amber beer has a big fluffy head of foam, and a rich sweet malt aroma with hints of citrus fruits and delicate hops. Rich malt dominates the mouth, while the finish is lingering, balanced between malt, fruit and hops.

■ **Doppelbock Dunkel (7% abv)**
In German, helles means pale or light, while dunkel means dark. This dunkel beer uses Munich malt, as well as pale lager malt, to produce a dark ruby-coloured beer. The beer has a thick, creamy head and a bready, yeasty, dark fruit (raisins and sultanas) aroma. The palate is reminiscent of rich fruit cake, while the finish, sweet to start, becomes dry and bitter with good hop notes from the Hallertauer hops.

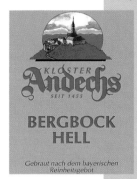

KLOSTER Andechs
SEIT 1455

BERGBOCK HELL

Gebraut nach dem bayerischen Reinheitsgebot

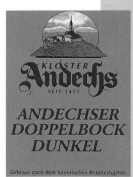

KLOSTER Andechs
SEIT 1455

ANDECHSER DOPPELBOCK DUNKEL

Gebraut nach dem bayerischen Reinheitsgebot

CONTACT

Klosterbräu Andechs • Kloster-strasse 1 • Andechs
Tel: 08152-1012 • www.andechs.de

weltenburg

Perched at the entrance to the Danube gorge, the Benedictine monastery of Weltenburg enjoys one of the finest locations in the world. It is also one of the oldest monastic breweries, having been brewing since the 11th century.

The monastery was founded in 610 by St. Eustace, a follower of the Irish missionary priest, St. Columbanus (see box, right) and a brewery was added sometime before 1050. The monks claim it is the oldest monastic brewery in the world. The monastery at Weihenstephan, near Munich, might have begun brewing earlier, but Weihenstephan was secularised in the 19th century while Weltenburg is still a monastery. Beer production has been interrupted only once in almost a thousand years, during the brief secularisation of the monastery after 1803.

THE ASAM BROTHERS

Vast numbers of visitors come to Weltenburg each year to marvel at the sumptuous architecture, the result of an 18th century redesign by the Asam brothers – great architects of the Baroque and among the foremost artists of their time. The monks were so overcome by the lavish and ornate nature of the design that they named the street alongside the monastery in honour of the architects and, more importantly, their Asam Doppelbock beer.

Columbanus: the merry saint

The founder of Weltenburg, St. Eustace, was a disciple of the 6th-century Irish missionary, St. Columbanus. In Columbanus, a love of God went hand-in-hand with a love of beer. We learn from his biographer, a monk called Jonas, that the saint once destroyed a tub full of beer, around which a group of pagans were ready to make a sacrifice, simply by blowing on it. Columbanus explained that God loved ale, but only when drunk in His name.

'It is my design to die in the brewhouse, let the ale be placed to my mouth when I am expiring so that when the choir of angels come they say: "Be God propitious to this drinker."'
St. Columbanus (543-615)

TASTING NOTES

Barock-Dunkel (4.5% abv)

A vast barley white head crowns this amber-red beer. There is a toasted malt aroma, dark malts and fruits in the mouth with a hint of chocolate, and a smoky, chewy finish.

Hefe-Weissbier Dunkel (5.1% abv)

This is a superb dark wheat beer with a creamy head. There is a nutty and fruity aroma, a spicy palate with hints of vanilla and fruit, and a long, dry finish dominated by rich dark malt.

Asam Doppelbock (6.5% abv)

A cappuccino-coloured head leads to a ruby-black beer with a malty and liquorice aroma. Dark malt, bitter chocolate and floral hops in the mouth, followed by a big finish dominated by toasted, smoky malt. Brewed with pale lager malt, Munich malt, caramalt and Hallertauer hops.

CONTACT

Klosterschenke Weltenburg • Asam-strasse 32 • Weltenburg
Tel: 09441-3682 • www.klosterschenke-weltenburg.de

spaten-franziskaner

The *Franziskaner* in the title of the company means Franciscan. Originally, Franziskaner was a wheat-beer brewery that stood alongside a Franciscan monastery in Munich and supplied the monks with their daily requirements.

The brewery was bought in 1861 by Joseph Sedlmayr, a member of the great Munich brewing dynasty that also owned Spaten. The two separate businesses merged in 1922 and the Franziskaner brewery closed in 1931, with production moved to Spaten. The brewery,

however, continues to produce the traditional wheat beers which the Franciscan monks once enjoyed. The Franciscan wheat beer now accounts for half of Spaten's production and the beer labels, with the image of a monk contemplating a tankard of beer, attest to the brewery's appreciation of its history. The Spaten brewery also produces a refreshing Oktoberfest beer: by tradition, the first to be tapped at the great Munich festival.

TASTING NOTES

■ **Helles Hefe-Weissbier (5% abv)**
A light wheat beer with a fruity, spicy, peppery aroma followed by rich banana and cloves in the mouth, with a long spicy, fruity, malty finish.

■ **Dunkel Hefe-Weissbier (5% abv)**
This dark wheat beer has a spicy, peppery aroma with a hint of chocolate. Creamy malt dominates the palate, with a finish balanced between peppery spiciness, dark toasted grain and chocolate.

■ **Oktoberfestbier (5.9% abv)**
A golden-coloured lager with a firm malty aroma and body balanced by floral hops and a hint of lemon citrus fruit.

THE WHEAT BEER REVIVAL

In recent years, wheat beer has undergone a resurgence in popularity. For young people, members of the 'green generation', wheat beer, especially in its cloudy, unfiltered form '*mit hefe*' (with yeast) is an uncomplicated, rustic type of beer that is healthier than conventional lagers made with barley. Certainly the live yeast, vitamins and proteins in wheat beer will contribute to good health if consumption is not overgenerous – one reason that monks originally drank the beer.

WEISSBIER

Wheat beers are warm-fermenting members of the ale family, with rich and enticing aromas and flavours reminiscent of apple, banana or cloves. The beers are all brewed with a proportion of barley malt as well as wheat malt. The reason is simple: barley has a husk that acts as a natural filter during the first mashing stage of the brewing process while wheat, lacking a husk, is far more difficult to brew with. The Franziskaner Weissbier has an unusually high wheat malt content of 75 per cent.

CONTACT

Spaten-Franziskaner-Bräu • 46-48 Mars-strasse • 80335 Munich
Tel: 089-51221 • www.spatenbraeu.de

austria

For centuries, Austria has been linked – geographically, historically and linguistically – with its bigger neighbour, Germany, and like Germany, Austria's breweries reflect the region's monastic heritage.

Only one of Austria's monasteries – at Schlägl – still brews beer today, but the many other breweries, like their monastic counterparts in Germany, continue to produce a variety of seasonal Bocks. Similarly, the Austrian breweries continue the monastic tradition of making strong Bock beers for the Christian Lent period. Austrian brewers played a pivotal role in the development of lagering, with the pioneering work of the Viennese brewer Anton Dreher, whose 'Vienna Red' style inspired the seasonal March beers of the Munich Oktoberfest (see box, page 75). Austria has also adopted from Switzerland a powerful Bock beer that celebrates Christmas and which faced extinction in its country of origin.

schloss-eggenberg

The brewery at Castle Eggenberg, in Austria, stands on the River Alm, between Linz and Salzburg, in an area of great beauty, with deep lakes, high mountains and dense forests. There has been a castle on the site since the 10th century, and the brewery there dates back to at least the 12th century, when the castle was owned by a local monastery. The castle has changed hands many times since, but the beers were first sold beyond the castle walls in 1681, when ownership passed from the monks of the Franciscan monastery of Kremsmünster into private hands. Today it's a fully fledged commercial operation run by the Stöhr family, who have owned the castle for almost two centuries. The castle and brewery were rebuilt in the 19th century, after being burned down in a fire, but the beer is still brewed with water from the spring that the medieval monks would have used. The brewery also retains a strong spiritual element: attached to the brewhouse is a small but exquisitely decorated chapel.

In spite of the small size of the brewery, it has achieved renown outside Austria. Eggenberg's Urbock 23, lagered for nine months in the castle's ancient cellars, is a fine rendition

Augustinerbräu

An Austrian brewery with a clear monastic link is Augustinerbräu in Salzburg, which is part-owned by a Benedictine settlement in nearby Michaelbeuern, although the brewery is run by professional brewers. The brewery has a beer hall, converted from an old monastery, and a beer garden, and produces both a March beer and a Bock.

of a Double Bock, full-bodied in the tradition of Bavaria's monastic brewers. The 23 refers to an old method of declaring the strength of beer and translates as 9.6% abv. Another world-renowned beer is MacQueen's Nessie Whisky Malt Red Beer, at 7.3% abv, which is brewed with whisky malt imported from Scotland.

SAMICHLAUS

Eggenberg's most intriguing speciality is a beer called Samichlaus, a powerful Swiss interpretation of the Bavarian Bock style. In the Swiss-German dialect, Samichlaus means Santa Claus. The beer was named Samichlaus because it was brewed every year on 6 December, St. Nicholas' Day, lagered for nine or ten months, before being bottled and released for the following year's celebrations (in Central Europe, St. Nicholas or Santa Claus appears

on 6 December, not just on Christmas Eve). At 14% abv, it has been awarded the title of the world's strongest regularly brewed beer, although this was not a title sought by the original brewers, the Hürlimann Brewery in Zürich, Switzerland, who first made the beer as part of scientific research into yeast.

TASTING NOTES

■ Samichlaus (14% abv)

A chestnut-coloured beer with an aroma of vinous fruit and spicy hops, with coffee, bitter chocolate, nuts and rich malt in the mouth, and a big, warming finish reminiscent of Cognac. Samichlaus is brewed with pale malts, together with three dark malts from France, Germany and Moravia. German Hallertauer, Hersbrucker and Styrian Goldings hops are used. Although the beer is filtered and pasteurised, the high level of alcohol means the beer will deepen in colour and improve with age.

schlägl

The Stiftsbrauerei Schlägl is the last remaining monastic brewery in Austria. The abbey, with its fine Baroque church and cloister, is situated in Upper Austria, the most important brewing region in the country, and close to the Czech border. Cistercian monks first began work on their settlement in 1218, and it seems reasonable to assume that brewing in the abbey began not long after. The monks, however, claim that the brewery was not founded until 1580, and since the cloisters contain an ancient library housing documents about the monastery, we should not dispute the brothers' modest claim.

The monastery's former lager cellars now house a brewery-restaurant. In addition, Schlägl uses a modern brewery, located opposite and run by lay workers — although the monks still have overall control. The monks claim that the brewing water, which is rich in calcium, flows to the well from the nearby Bohemian Forest.

A NOURISHING BREW

Like the Bavarian monastic breweries, the abbey at Schlägl also brews a Double Bock: a modern beer, but one in the tradition of those

CONTACT

Schlossbrauerei Eggenberg • Postfach 44 • A-4655 Vorchdorf • Austria
Tel 07614 345 • www.schlosseggenberg.at

Vienna Red beers

Schlägl also produces a now rare example of a speciality known as Märzen or March beer, first created when a 19th-century Viennese brewer, Anton Dreher, sought to brew a beer inspired by the first dark lagers in Munich. He used slightly paler malts to produce an amber beer that became known as 'Vienna Red'. This inspired a Munich brewer to also brew an amber lager which he dubbed Märzen, as it was brewed in March, stored until the autumn, and then broached at the Oktoberfest. The beer can be seen as a modern descendent of the seasonal beers made by the medieval brewers, brewed in March before the warm summer weather made brewing impossible.

Vienna Red lagers all but disappeared from Austria, while even in Munich, March beers have been largely replaced by paler beers brewed specifically for the Oktoberfest. The brewery at Schlägl, however, continues to produce this classic Austrian speciality.

once brewed by medieval monks to be consumed during fasts, or to supplement their simple diets – full bodied, satisfying and strong. Schlägl's bready Doppelbock is a fine example of the style, using hops grown in the surrounding fields, and matured for 12 weeks in icy, stone lager cellars. The monastic brewery is also well known for its Golden Roggen, a warm-fermented beer that is brewed with rye as well as barley malt.

TASTING NOTES

■ Doppelbock (7% abv)

An amber-coloured beer made with pale and Vienna malts, and local hops. There is a rich malty-bready aroma, a firm malt-dominated body with gentle hop bitterness, and a dry finish where hops balance the sweet malt. The yeasty, bready character of the beer points up the old monks' description of this style as 'liquid bread'.

CONTACT

Stiftsbrauerei Schlägl • Schlägl 1 • A-4160 Aigen-Schlägl • Austria
Tel: 07281 8801 • www.schlaegl.co.at

switzerland

The small alpine country of Switzerland has a long and noble brewing tradition that dates back to the medieval abbey of St. Gall, one of the earliest and greatest of Europe's monastic breweries.

■ Schützengarten

In the 7th century AD, an Irish Benedictine monk named Gall helped to introduce not only Christianity and learning to Switzerland but also the skills to make beer, and the abbey that was founded in his name became one of the earliest large-scale breweries that we know of today (see box, page 10). The canton of Gallen, which was named in his honour, is close to the border with Germany, and the beer produced in Switzerland today has been greatly influenced by Germanic brewing methods. Unfortunately, Switzerland lost many of its independent breweries – including the scientifically distinguished brewery of Hürlimann – as they rushed to merge in the 20th century. One of Hürlimann's most renowned beers, Samichlaus, has since been adopted by the Austrian brewery of Schloss-Eggenberg (see page 72). The brewery of Schützengarten, however, not only survives as heir to the brewing monks of St. Gall, but commemorates its predecessors with an abbey beer of the same name.

schützengarten

The only surviving major brewery in the canton of Gallen, where the great monastic brewery of that name once stood, Schützengarten is also the country's oldest beer producer, founded in 1779. The centuries seem few, however, when compared to the venerable and distinguished history of brewing in the region. The brewery began by making wheat beers, until the lager revolution a century later prompted it to switch most of its products to cold fermentation. It still produces a wheat beer – an unfiltered, cloudy brew whose nourishing qualities the medieval monks of St. Gall might well have appreciated. With this wheat beer, the St. Galler Landbier, and a rich, unfiltered lager called St. Galler Klosterbrau, the brewery pays tribute to the beers once brewed in the cloisters of the great medieval monastery.

TASTING NOTES

■ St. Galler Landbier (5% abv)

An unfiltered, cloudy-yellow wheat beer with a ripe aroma of banana and cloves, a palate dominated by fruit and spices, and a lingering finish with fruit, spices and gentle hops. Made with pale malt, wheat malt, and German Hallertauer and Czech Saaz hops.

■ St. Galler Klosterbräu (5.2% abv)

An amber-coloured, hazy beer with a rich yeasty-bready aroma, a big malty and hoppy palate, and a long finish balanced between rich grain, bitter hops and some light fruit. This unfiltered beer is brewed with pale and amber malts, and German Hallertauer and Czech Saaz hops.

CONTACT

Brauerei Schützengarten • St. Jakobstrasse 37
St. Gallen • Switzerland • Tel 071-243 43 43
www.schuetzengarten.ch

CHRISTMAS BEERS

The mid-winter period has been a time for drinking and festivities since pagan times, and brewers have long celebrated Christmas with beers brewed specially for the season.

Pagan celebrations to mark the winter solstice – the Yuletide – were accompanied by copious quantities of strong ale, both for imbibing during the feasts, and for offering as a libation to the gods. When these pagan festivals were adopted by the Christian church to mark the birth of Christ ('Christ's mass' was set to coincide with the height of the solstice festivities), the consumption of ale continued to be an integral part of the feasting and carousing that accompanied the Christmas period. Naturally, the monastic breweries were at the forefront of these celebrations, brewing special ales for drinking during the festivities.

Today, many breweries contribute to celebrate the season of good cheer with beers brewed specifically for the occasion. Christmas is a chance to introduce spicy, fruity, seasonal flavours to the beers, bringing the welcome warmth of alcohol to the depths of winter.

ST. NIKOLAUS BOCK
Penn Brewing, USA

Penn's 8.4% abv St. Nikolaus Bock is both a brilliant interpretation of dark Bock and a fine contribution to the Christmas season. It's rich and dark in colour with roasted grain and chocolate on the aroma, full-bodied malt and light hop notes in the mouth, followed by a long finish dominated by roasted grain, chocolate and delicate hops.

HET ELFDE GEBOD
Arcen Brewery, the Netherlands

This 7% abv beer is a cheering beer for Christmas in every possible way: the name means 'the Eleventh Commandment', a light-hearted invitation for the Dutch to eat and drink well. This may not be the most pious of the commandments – the label shows a devil tempting a reclining woman – but the beer sits well with the convivial, indulgent spirit of the season. It has an enticing gold colour, and rich apple-like fruit on the aroma, balanced by delicate hops. There's biscuity malt and tart fruit in the mouth, and a finish that starts sweet and malty but which becomes dry and bitter with a good underpinning of rich fruit.

GRANDE RÉSERVE
Chimay, Belgium

The 9% abv Grande Réserve, from the biggest and best-known of the Belgian Trappist breweries, is an ideal beer for the Christmas season. The beer has a fruitiness that marries well with the foods prepared for the festivities. It has a deep copper colour and a vast fruit character on the aroma, with spiciness from hops and yeast. The palate is rich and fruity

while the finish becomes dry with spicy hops. The Grande Réserve is bottle-fermented, and so is ideal for storing to drink on special occasions.

CHRISTMAS SPINGO SPECIAL
Blue Anchor, England

The seasonal beers produced by this world-famous brew-pub bring crowds flocking to the tiny inn – never more so than for the spicy Christmas Special. The potent ale has a dark ruby colour and an earthy, blackcurrant aroma balanced by spicy hops. Dry fruit and malt in the mouth is followed by a long fruity finish with vanilla, caramel and peppery hops. It's usually 7.6% abv but the strength can vary: drinkers have to be wary that extra strong versions do not prolong the Christmas holiday by several days!

SAMICHLAUS
Schloss-Eggenberg, Austria

A classic Christmas beer brewed to celebrate the feast of St. Nicholas (better known in English as Santa Claus – or Samichlaus in Swiss-German dialect), this beer is firmly in the tradition of the medieval monks who brewed celebratory beers for their religious festivals. At 14% abv it is one of the world's strongest beers: quite strong enough to warm the body and impart a heady dose of Christmas cheer. It is a chestnut-coloured beer with an aroma of vinous fruit and spicy hops. There is coffee, bitter chocolate, nuts and rich malt in the mouth, followed by a warming, Cognac-like finish.

czech republic

Bohemia, in the Czech Republic, holds a special, iconic place in the annals of brewing. It was in Pilsen, the powerhouse of the Bohemian industrial revolution, that the first golden lager beer appeared, and transformed brewing worldwide.

■ Klásterni Pivovar

Today, nearly all the major breweries in the republic make Pilsen-type golden beers, though a few dark beers of the Munich style survive. Even the brewers of Ceské Budejovice, a town founded by monks in the 13th century, are renowned today for golden lager beer (their excellent Budweiser beer has been the cause of endless court battles with the giant American corporation that brews a beer of the same name). But Bohemia has an older tradition.

It may even be that we owe the adoption of hops in brewing – one of the great innovations in brewing history – to the region's brewers, who were growing hops as far back as the 9th century. Across the Czech Republic, brewing is still centred around small village breweries, many making beer in a manner unchanged for centuries – even in Prague, the monastic tradition has begun to resurface since the fall of Communism.

klásterní pivovar

The Cloister Brewery – *Klásterni Pivovar* in Czech – is attached to the magnificant Baroque abbey of Strahov, on Petrin Hill in Prague. First built in the 12th century, both abbey and brewery were destroyed during the Hussite wars in the 14th century. When the abbey was rebuilt in 1515, King Vladislav Jagellon restored the monks' brewing rights. A century later, a new brewery was built opposite the abbey, although it was badly damaged during the Thirty Years War, when it was occupied by Swedish troops.

The brewery was repaired in 1759 and survived until 1919, shortly after the birth of the Czechoslovak nation.

In July 2000 the abbey's old brewhouse was restored and reopened as a brewery-restaurant. The privately owned Klásterni brewery, which rents the buildings from the abbey, produces two beers. Both are named Svaty Norbert in honour of the 12th century founder of the monastic order of Prémontré, whose body and relics are housed in Strahov Abbey today.

TASTING NOTES

■ Svaty Norbert Pale 12 (5.2% abv)
A hazy gold beer with a pronounced juicy
malt and citrus hop nose, with malt and
hops dominating the palate, followed by a
bitter-sweet finish that finally becomes dry
and hoppy with lemon fruit notes. Made
with pale Moravian malt and Saaz hops.
The Svaty Norbert beers are not
pasteurised and the Pale has a slight haze.

■ Svaty Norbert Dark 14 (6.2% abv)
Ruby-black beer with a big chocolate aroma
balanced by spicy hops, roasted grain in
the mouth with more chocolate notes, and a
long creamy malt finish with fig-like
fruitiness. Brewed with three Moravian
malts, one Bavarian malt and Saaz hops.

CONTACT

Klásterni Pivovar • Strahovské Nadvori 302
118 00 Prague • www.klasterni-pivovar.cz

england

Beer has been a part of English life for centuries, and until their dissolution in the 16th century, the brewing industry was dominated by monasteries. But old habits die hard: even today, many breweries retain some tantalizing links with the past.

When the Normans invaded England in the 11th century, they found brewing so deeply ingrained in the local way of life that they did not attempt to impose their own preference for wine and cider. The 1086 Domesday Book census found 43 *cerevisiarii* (commercial brewers), in addition to the domestic home brewing that was prevalent at this time. Such was the demand for beer, the Domesday book states that a brewer could be fined four shillings or ducked in the village pond if he made bad ale.

But these cerevisiarii also faced serious competition from the Church; the Domesday Book shows that breweries, such as those in Fountains Abbey, were capable of producing large amounts of ale each year. Many smaller monasteries also had breweries, producing beer for the monks and for the outside world. Motives were not entirely altruistic: by cornering the manufacture and supply of ale, the Church could boost the income of the abbeys and monasteries.

A MEDIEVAL INDUSTRY

Monastic brewhouses could be vast in scale. The malt house at Fountains Abbey in Yorkshire measured almost 50 square metres and the brewhouse produced 60 barrels of strong ale every 10 days. The Domesday Book recorded that the monks of St. Paul's Cathedral in London brewed about 1,880 barrels a year.

THE END OF THE MONASTIC BREWERS

The dissolution of the monasteries by Henry VIII (pictured, left) not only broke the power of Rome in England – and eased the king's marital and financial problems – but also ended monastic brewing, paving the way for the development of a modern brewing industry. But the monasteries still influence us. In breweries large and small, there are still fascinating links with brewing methods of centuries ago and, in some cases, even attempts to recreate ales that might please a monk in the 14th century.

marston's

The roots of brewing in Burton date back a millennium, to the founding of Burton Abbey in 1002. The Benedictine monks discovered that the water which bubbled to the surface from hundreds of natural springs was ideal for producing good ale. The monks who brewed at the abbey set in train a course of events that was to turn Burton, by the 19th century, into the capital of British brewing, renowned throughout the world for its India Pale Ales. The monks also inspired a method of fermentation still used at Marston's today.

Miraculous water

The spring water used by Burton's brewing monks was analysed and found to contain high levels of salts, in particular calcium sulphate (gypsum) and magnesium. These salts encourage a powerful fermentation, helping to extract the oils and resins from hops, and giving the finished beer a tempting sparkle and a refreshing quality.

Marston, Thompson & Evershed began to brew beer in Burton in 1834 and moved to its present-day site, the red-brick Albion Brewery, in 1898. It was around this time that glass began to replace pewter and leather, so that for the first time drinkers could see what they were drinking, and many were unimpressed with murky, yeasty beers. A consistent method of cleansing beer of yeast was vital to the success of pale ale. It was not an easy problem to resolve, for yeast remained in suspension during fermentation. Peter Walker, a Merseyside brewer who briefly owned a site in Burton, came to the rescue. His stroke of genius was to take a medieval method of fermentation devised by monks and turn it on its head.

THE BURTON UNION SYSTEM
Today, only Marston's brewery remains true to Walker's system. The brewery is based round giant wooden casks, each one holding 144

Museum Brewing Company

This brewery, based in the Bass museum in the heart of Burton, is dedicated to the recreation of old Bass beers using recipes kept in the company's archives. In 2001 the company introduced Wulfric, a bottle-fermented beer that commemorates Wulfric Spott, the Earl of Mercia, who funded the building of Burton Abbey in 1002. The amber-coloured beer is a modern one that uses hops, although the plant was unknown to brewers in England in the 11th century and all manner of herbs, plants and spices were used to balance the sweetness of malt. As a gesture to this ancient heritage, Wulfric is brewed with some ginger essence.

gallons of liquid, that are linked by pipes and troughs – or 'held in union', as the Victorians said. Whereas monks had allowed the fermenting liquid (known as wort) to gush from oak casks into troughs placed on the ground – a hit-and-miss, messy affair – Walker placed troughs above the fermentation casks and linked them using swan-necked pipes. The troughs were positioned with a slight incline. As a result, the fermenting liquid ran down the troughs and then back into the cask, while most of the yeast was held back. By the time fermentation was complete, most of the yeast had been collected in the troughs, leaving clear liquid behind in the casks. Today, only one brand, Marston's Pedigree Bitter, is produced in the union casks. It is one of the country's leading real ales and is a living testimony to the enduring impact of monastic brewing from centuries ago.

TASTING NOTES

■ Marston's Pedigree Bitter (4.5% abv)

A pale-copper colour, this bitter is made with pale malt, glucose, and Fuggles and Goldings whole hops. The aroma at first is dominated by a powerful sulphury note, like a freshly struck Swan Vesta match, which comes from the salts in the brewing water: the aroma is known as 'the Burton snatch'. As the sulphur clears, malt, hops and delicate apple fruit appear on the nose. The apple note was typical of all Burton pale ales brewed in the union system. Malt, hops and fruit linger on the tongue, while the finish, after an initial burst of malt and fruit, becomes increasingly bitter from the hops, with a slight touch of saltiness from the water.

CONTACT

Marston • Thompson & Evershed PLC • The Brewery • Shobnall Road
Burton-on-Trent • Staffs DE14 2BW • Tel: 01283 531131 • www.breworld.com/marstons

Brakspear

W.H. Brakspear, which enjoys an idyllic location close to the banks of the River Thames at Henley, has a powerful family link with the only Englishman to hold the office of Pope. While the brewing family changed the spelling of its surname from Breakspear to Brakspear in the late 18th century, it is related to Nicholas Breakspear who, as Adrian IV, became Pope in 1154. Pope Adrian incorporated the symbol of a bee in his mitre to mark the fact that the first letter of the family name was 'B'. Today, the bee is the trade-mark of the brewery.

Brakspear became a limited company early in the 20th century and a PLC in the 1980s, but the majority of shares are still controlled by the family. Many shares are owned by employees and retired workers who still live in the Henley area. In July 2002 the company

> "What two ideas are more inseperable that Beer and Britannia?"
>
> *Rev. Sydney Smith (1771-1845)*

Thomas à Becket

Nicholas Breakspear was educated at the Augustinian priory of Merton, where he may have come into contact with Thomas à Becket, another of England's most distinguished churchmen. In 1158, when Becket led a diplomatic mission to France, he took with him two wagons laden with iron-bound casks of ale. According to a contemporary report the French,

'wondered at such an invention – a drink most wholesome, clear of all dregs, rivalling wine in colour and surpassing it in savour'

CONTACT

W H Brakspear & Sons PLC • The Brewery • New Street • Henley-on-Thames • Oxon RG9 2BU
Tel: 01491 570200 • www.brakspear.co.uk

TASTING NOTES

■ Bitter (3.4% abv)

Brakspear Bitter is made with Maris Otter pale malt, Pipkin crystal and black malt, and Fuggles, Goldings and Styrian Goldings hops. An aroma of wholemeal biscuits and orange peel is followed by malt and floral hops in the mouth and a dry finish dominated by massive hop notes.

■ Special (4% abv)

Using the same ingredients as the Bitter, the Special enjoys a rich malt, hops and fruit aroma. This is followed by a ripe and rounded palate with tart fruit and malt dominating. The finish is bittersweet with orange and banana fruit notes.

announced plans to close the Henley brewery, much to the distress of lovers of its fine pale ales. The beers will continue to be sold in Brakspear's pubs in the Thames Valley. The beers will be brewed temporarily under licence elsewhere, but there are plans to build a new site as close to Henley as possible.

st. peter's

St. Peter's Brewery, based in an imposing medieval farmhouse in Suffolk, produces a fascinating beer named King Cnut, after the 11th-century Danish ruler of England. The beer is an attempt to recreate a genuine ale from 1,000 years ago, and comes closer than any to reproducing the taste of an early monastic beer.

It uses no hops, which were unknown at the time, but balances the sweetness of malt with juniper and stinging nettles: hops come from the same plant family as nettles.

TASTING NOTES

■ King Cnut Ale (5% abv)

A dark, ruby-brown ale, with a smoky, nutty, roasted grain aroma overlain by a powerful waft of juniper. The palate is tart and spicy with hints of rhubarb fruit. The finish is dry, bitter, spicy, fruity and peppery. Ingredients include Halcyon pale malt, roasted barley, juniper and stinging nettles.

CONTACT

St. Peter's Hall • St. Peter South Elmham • Bungay • Suffolk NR35 1NQ • Tel: 01986 782322 • www.stpetersbrewery.co.uk

nethergate

Nethergate Brewery is a comparatively new small craft brewery, set up in 1986 in the old Suffolk market town of Clare. The town also has an Augustinian priory that was founded in 1248, the first to be built by followers of St. Augustine of Hippo, one of the greatest thinkers of the Christian Church. The Clare priory became the mother house of the Order of Augustinian Friars in England until it was dissolved in 1538. Fifty years ago, Augustinian friars returned to Clare and the old infirmary became a permanent church. Four Augustinian brothers now live on the site, which has once again become a place of retreat.

In 1998, to commemorate the 750th anniversary of the founding of the priory, Nethergate brewed a beer called Augustinian Ale with the agreement of the prior, who receives a royalty on the sales of the beer.

TASTING NOTES

■ **Draught cask-conditioned Augustinian Ale (4.8% abv)**
Made with Maris Otter pale malt, crystal malt and Styrian Goldings hops, this draught version has a fruity-hoppy aroma with a full palate dominated by rich malt, spicy hops and a touch of citrus fruit. A long and complex finish is balanced between malt, fruit and hops. The beer is a pale-amber colour.

■ **Bottle fermented Augustinian Ale (5.2% abv)**
Made with similar ingredients to the draught, the addition of crushed coriander seeds give it a powerful, heady aroma of coriander with an underpinning of soft malt. There are rich malt, hops and spices in the mouth, with a lingering finish dominated by coriander, fruity hops and creamy malt.

CONTACT

Nethergate Brewery • 11–13 High Street • Clare • Suffolk CO10 8NY
Tel: 01787 277244

WINTER BEERS

Throughout history, beer has played a vital role during the cold winter months, comforting and sustaining, a role reflected in many of the rich, strong winter beers available today.

For the medieval monks of Northern Europe, particularly the Bavarian monastic brewers in their chilly cloisters deep in the Alps, winter was a time of biting cold, short days and stark – sometimes beautiful – countryside. It was also a period of hardship and discomfort. The beers they brewed to support them through these long winter months needed to be rich and nourishing, to warm the heart and the soul.

Today, our lives are far more comfortable, but we continue to appreciate these qualities in winter beers. Whatever the region, beers have to deliver warmth, richness and a degree of comfort. Winter beers are for sipping rather than quaffing, ideally in front of a roaring fire, and either drunk on their own or accompanied by a warming pie, strong, tangy cheese or nuts.

DOPPELBOCK
Stiftsbrauerei Schlägl, Austria

This 7% abv Doppelbock from the only remaining monastery brewery in Upper Austria is a splendidly rich and warming beer well suited for the cold Alpine winters. It has an amber colour, and a yeasty and bready character with rich, juicy malt dominating the mouth, followed by a dry finish with a lingering hint of delicate hops.

QUADRUPEL
La Trappe, the Netherlands

At 10% abv, the Quadrupel produced in the commercial brewery alongside Koningshoeven Abbey is a mighty beer, one that is perfect for the winter period. It is red-bronze in colour, with rich orange fruit on the aroma balanced by spicy hops, biscuity malt, spices and hops in the mouth, and a long, satisfyingly smooth finish with creamy malt, gentle spices, delicate hops and warming alcohol. Like many of the Trappist monasteries, the monks of Koningshoeven also oversee the production of a malty, abbey cheese, matured and seasoned with La Trappe beer, an excellent accompaniment to the Quadrupel on a cold winter's day.

DUBBELBOCK
Brand Brewing, the Netherlands

This powerful, 7.5% abv Dutch Bock has a port wine colour, a deep aroma of vinous fruit, floral hops and chocolate, with creamy malt and dark fruit dominating the mouth, and a rich fruity finish balanced by chocolate and spicy hops.

ABBEY ALE
Ommegang, USA

This rich, complex Abbey Ale (8.5% abv) comes from an American craft brewery specializing in Belgian-style ales. It has a burgundy colour, with fruit, hops and spices on the aroma, a palate rich in caramel, liquorice, toffee, chocolate and hops, and a dry finish with citrus fruits, peppery hops and rich grain. A winter feast all on its own.

WULFRIC
Museum Brewery, England

This is an English interpretation of the bottle-conditioned, spicy, abbey beers drunk through the winter in Belgium. It is brewed to in honour of Wulfric Earl of Mercia, who founded Burton Abbey in the 11th century, helping to establish the great brewing town of Burton. Although it is not strong for a winter beer, at only 5.5% abv, ginger is used in the recipe, giving a wonderfully warming, mulled character to the beer. There is ginger on the aroma, balanced by hops and fruit. Peppery hops dominate the palate, with ginger flavours in the background, and lingering hops and ginger in the finish.

ABBEY TRIPLE
Stoudt's, USA

Stoudt's Abbey Triple (9% abv) has a welcoming warming character. The appellation 'Triple' is a reference to the strong Trappist beers brewed by the monks for drinking on special occasions such as the Christmas festivities, and Stoudt's Triple is certainly a beer to put some cheer into the winter season. It has an orange colour with spicy hops and rich malt on the aroma, a firm malty body rich in alcohol, and a big, lingering finish with spicy hops, ripe malt and tart fruit.

theakston

The Theakston brewery, which first started brewing in the ancient market town of Masham in 1827, produces one of the best-known and curiously named strong beers in Britain: 'Old Peculier'. Old Peculier belongs to the style known as 'old ale' – rich, complex, bitter-sweet beers that were once matured in oak casks for long periods.

The court seal

The chairman of the Peculier Court had a great seal made that was used to stamp his approval on decisions made by the court. The symbol is used today for all Theakston's beer. The kneeling figure is believed to be Roger de Mowbray, a local knight who was captured while on crusade. Released from captivity by the Knights Templar, de Mowbray allowed the Archbishopric of York control over the church at Masham in gratitude. The seal depicts him as prisoner in the Holy Land.

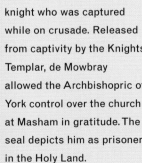

Driven by the national fame of Old Peculier, Theakston became a small brewery with a big reputation in the 1970s and 80s. The brewing process is still carried out in splendidly traditional vessels, and the finest English malts and hops are used for aroma and flavour.

The brewery also houses a local museum and visitors' centre, offering a fascinating journey back to the brewing methods of the 19th century. There is even a coopers' shop where wooden beer casks are still fashioned in the time-honoured way, using tools handed down through generations of craftsmen. The casks are used to deliver the draught version of Old Peculier to certain pubs 'in the wood'.

THE PECULIER COURT

The word 'peculier' (meaning particular rather than odd) comes from the turbulent period of the 11th and 12th centuries. Masham at the time was just a small village and reaching it meant a long and difficult journey into the Dales, where vagabonds and cut-throats waited to rob and kill travellers. The Archbishop of York made an order freeing Masham 'of all the customs and claims of his archdeacons and officials' and established an independent ecclesiastical court, the Peculier Court of Masham, to administer law in the area.

The court still sits today. Composed of '24 good men from the parish', the chairman is the Vicar of Masham. The crimes punishable by the Peculier Court include 'drunkenness, keeping a

hat on during communion, harbouring Catholic priests, brawling, swearing, scolding, not bringing your children to be baptised, bidding church wardens to do their worst when they order you to church and carrying a skull out of a churchyard to lay under a person's head to charm him or her to sleep'. The last malpractice is not thought to occur regularly these days.

TASTING NOTES

■ Old Peculier (5.7% abv)

Made with pale malt, crystal malt and brewing sugar, together with Fuggles and other varieties of whole hops. The ale has a big vinous aroma of rich raisin-like fruit with peppery hop notes. Toffee and roast malt dominate the mouth, followed by a deep, bitter-sweet finish with a good underpinning of spicy hop notes.

CONTACT

T&R Theakston Ltd • Wellgarth • Masham • Ripon • North Yorkshire HG4 4YD
Tel: 01765 680000 • www.theakstons.co.uk

Blue Anchor

Originally a monastery hospice, ale has been made on the site of the Blue Anchor inn at Helston, Cornwall, for around 600 years. Monks built a hospice at Helston because it had a well with a plentiful supply of fresh water, but beer was preferred, as even spring water could contain cholera or typhus viruses.

The dissolution of the monasteries in the 1530s was wide-reaching in its brutality. Even the small and humble hospice in Helston was closed. It became a village inn and, since Helston was an important port, took on the name of Blue Anchor. Today, the inn remains gloriously unspoilt and enjoys protected status as a Grade One listed building.

TASTING NOTES

■ Middle Spingo (5% abv)

Made with pale malt and Goldings hops, Middle Spingo has a deep copper-red colour and little foam. The ale has a big fruity aroma of raisins and sultanas with a hint of vanilla and an earthy, peppery note from the hops. There is a nutty, fruitcake palate. The long bitter-sweet finish, with a raspberry-like fruitiness, is balanced by the dryness of the hops.

■ Spingo Special (6.6% abv)

Also made with pale malt and Goldings hops, Spingo Special is similar to Spingo Middle, with a slightly darker colour and a pronounced earthy character on the nose, balanced by rich fruit. Fruit and peppery hops dominate the mouth, followed by a big finish in which malt, fruit and hops vie for attention.

■ Christmas/Easter Special (7.6% abv)

Dark ruby in colour with a massive earthy and blackcurrant fruit aroma, balanced by spicy hops. Dry fruit and malt dominate the mouth while the finish is long and fruity with hints of vanilla, caramel and peppery hops.

The Blue Anchor brews powerful ales called Spingo. With the exception of hops, the beers may not be so different to those made by the monks 600 years ago. They are certainly reputed to have remarkable restorative powers, even encouraging the Blue Anchor to gain repute as a Cornish version of Lourdes. The present landlord once found a pair of crutches abandoned in the pub garden. 'Someone must have come in with them,' he says, 'but they certainly didn't leave with them.'

Bragget: The Celtic beer

The Blue Anchor brews a rich, golden ale called Spingo 800, based on an ancient Celtic beer style known as Bragget, which was made without hops. Brewed with pale malt, honey and apple juice, and using the earthy-spicy house yeast, the ale may come close to recreating the type of beer once brewed in medieval English monasteries.

CONTACT

Blue Anchor • 50 Coinagehall Street • Helston • Cornwall
Tel: 01326 562821

greene king

A monastery was founded in Bury St. Edmunds as early as the 7th century. King Canute (or Cnut) established a Benedictine community in 1020 to commemorate St. Edmund, slain by the Danes in the 9th century. The place became known as St. Edmundsbury, which became the modern town of Bury St. Edmunds.

The Domesday Book records that monks brewed ale at the abbey in St. Edmundsbury as early as the 11th century. Monks were entitled to a gallon (4.5 litres) of beer a day, increasing to a gallon-and-a-half when ill.

Greene King is a comparatively modern brewing company, dating from the late 18th century, but it has connections with the monks of St. Edmundsbury that go beyond the name of its best-known beer, Abbot Ale. When Benjamin Greene bought Wright's Brewery on Westgate in 1799, he also moved into the impressive mansion that had been the secular home of the last Abbot of Bury. Greene, with a sharper eye for business than for history, pulled down the mansion in 1854 to enable his brewery to expand.

A rival brewery owned by Frederick King opened on Westgate in 1868. As brewers throughout the country went on a wild spending spree to buy pubs and establish 'tied

St. Edmund's Ale

Greene King produce a house speciality called St. Edmund's Ale, inspired by the life – and death – of the 9th-century martyr. After being captured by the Danes in AD 870, King Edmund was tortured and beheaded. When his followers found his torso, they searched in vain for his head until finally they heard a voice crying, 'Here! Here!' They dashed into the woods, and found Edmund's head between the paws of a giant wolf. When the head was placed on the torso, they miraculously joined together again. The credibility of this story is aided by a generous consumption of the ale.

trade' outlets that served only the products of the owning breweries, Greene and King became fierce rivals. In 1887 they merged with a joint tied estate of 148 pubs. Today, Greene King is a brewing giant in England with an estate of more than 1,600 pubs.

ABBOT ALE

While the main product of the brewery is a standard bitter called IPA, the beer that has built the brewery's reputation since its introduction in 1955 is Abbot Ale, a robust, characterful beer. The ale is fermented for a full eight days; giving the beer two sabbaths ensures that it is 'twice blessed'.

TASTING NOTES

■ Abbot Ale (5% abv)

Made with Pipkin and Halcyon pale malts, crystal malt, amber malt and brewing sugar, Abbot Ale also contains a small amount of caramel for colour adjustment, giving the ale a distinct copper shade. There is a big aroma of ripe fruit and tart hops (Challenger, Northdown and Target hops are all used), rich malt and fruit in the mouth, and an intense bittersweet finish.

■ St. Edmund's Ale (5.5% abv)

This pale bronze-coloured beer uses pale and crystal malts, and Target hops, and has a rich malty aroma with a hint of vanilla. Sweet malt and peppery hops dominate the mouth, followed by a bittersweet finish with nutty malt and peppery hops to the fore.

CONTACT

Greene King PLC • Abbot House • Westgate Brewery • Bury St. Edmunds • Suffolk IP33 1QT
Tel: 01284 763222 • www.greeneking.com

íRelaᚐᚋᚐ

The Irish fondness for a glass of beer – or, to be more precise, a glass of stout – can be traced to the founding father, St. Patrick, the missionary priest who converted the Irish to Christianity in the 5th century.

■ Celtic Brew

■ Smithwick's

St. Patrick is believed to have employed his own brewer, a sensible precaution at a time when water was undrinkable unless boiled. Many other Irish saints, from St. Brigid to St. Columba, are celebrated for their love of ale, and the beer brewed by Irish monks has long enjoyed a reputation outside their own country. As far back as the first century AD, a historian named Dioscorides noted that 'the Hiberni [Irish], instead of wine use a liquor called courmi or curmi, made of barley.'

The deep roots that Catholicism still has in Ireland have not saved this monastic brewing tradition: under English rule, the monasteries were dissolved just as brutally as in England. Brewing in Ireland today is a modern business using state-of-the-art methods. The reason is simple: anyone who dares to brew in Ireland does so in the giant shadow cast by Guinness. Intriguingly, the church did play an early role in the story of Guinness, when the founder was left £100 by the rector of Celbridge, enabling him to buy his first brewery.

Irish brewing may be a largely secular affair today, but Ireland's great heritage is far from being forgotten. In Kilkenny and in County Meath breweries exist that still proudly proclaim their monastic inheritance.

celtic BReᚒ

Based on the site of a great 6th-century monastery, Celtic Brew is one of Ireland's fastest-growing craft breweries. The monastery was founded by St. Finian, an early Irish bishop and missionary, between the ancient kingdoms of Meath and Leinster. Finian was a great scholar, and the monastery at Clonard rapidly became one of the most important schools of learning of the age, for a time second only to Rome as a centre of Christian life. The monastery at Clonard survived until the 12th century, when Norman colonists from across the Irish Sea allowed this once-great centre of Irish religious life to fall into terminal decline.

ST. FINIAN'S WELL

One of St. Finian's first steps, when founding the monastery, was to sink a well from which to draw water for the brothers. Legend has it that he was visited soon after this by an angel, who instructed him to move the well. The site of the new well remains a focus for pilgrimage today, and there is little doubt that its water was once used in the making of beer. Brewing artefacts and implements discovered in the remains of the monastery suggest the site not only had its own brewery, but may even have had its own school of brewing – probably the first formal centre for brewing education in the British Isles. The abbey at Clonard may even have influenced the development of brewing on mainland Europe, as travellers and pilgrims who rested there took knowledge of the monk's brewing skills back home.

A CELTIC REVIVAL

The Anglo-Norman invasions were not the last time that Catholic-Irish traditions were to come under threat from colonialism. Celtic Brew has set out to revive the true Irish Catholic brewing tradition suppressed during the centuries of the British ascendancy when Catholic monasteries were wrecked and ransacked, and commercial brewing was dominated by Protestants. The Irish wolfhounds used on its logo are based on one of the three devices on the crest of the High Kings of Ireland.

Opened in 1997 by the then Irish Taoiseach (prime minister), the brewery's success is measured by the fact that it quickly outgrew its initial capacity. It has doubled its output every year since. As well as Finian's Irish Stout, Celtic also brews an Irish Red Ale. This ale is the oldest beer style in Ireland – predating the porters and stouts of the 18th century by several hundred years – and has the closest links to the type of ales once brewed in monasteries.

■ Finian's Irish Stout (4.3% abv)
Brewed with pale, crystal, roasted and stout malts, and Irish Northdown hops, this stout is a jet-black colour with a ruby edge, topped by dense barley-white foam. Roasted malt and liquorice on the aroma are followed by a palate dominated by bitter grain and hops, and an intensely dry and bitter finish, with iodine-like hoppiness and bitter dark grain and tart fruit.

■ Finian's Irish Red Ale (4.6% abv)
A red-bronze beer with a snowy white collar of foam, and a roasted malt, marzipan, sappy wood and hop resin aroma. Sweet juicy malt in the mouth is balanced by tart hops, and followed by a lingering, distinctive finish that starts with creamy, roasted malt and hints of vanilla but becomes dry and bitter. A hoppy-bitter interpretation of the style, it is made with pale, crystal and roast malts, with German Hersbrucker and Irish Northdown hops.

St. Brigid
One Irish saint with a miraculous connection to beer is the 5th-century abbess, St. Brigid, who is reputed to have turned her bathwater into ale to satisfy the thirst of an unexpected visitor. Brigid seems to have been fond of the brew herself: a poem attributed to the saint begins with the lines

'I should like a great lake of beer for the king of kings, I should like the angels of heaven to be drinking it through time eternal.'

CONTACT

Celtic Brew • Enfield • Co Meath • Tel: 04 044 1558

smithwick's

Kilkenny, a thriving market town with an imposing Norman castle, was the seat of the Irish parliament in the 13th century. The city started life as a humble monastic settlement, and the name Kilkenny developed from Canice, the monks' leader, who is commemorated by St. Canice Cathedral. The medieval abbey around which Smithwick's brewery is now built was founded sometime after 1231, and became an important Franciscan abbey after the arrival of the friars in Ireland in 1266. Brewing at the site almost certainly dates back to the Franciscan friars, who would have brewed ale to sustain their life and work.

THE SECULAR BREWERY

The abbey was dissolved in the 16th century and the friars expelled. The abbey was rededicated under James I but was in such a poor state of repair that it could not be used. The tower and nave are all that are left. In 1706 a grant was given to Richard Cole to build a new brewery in the grounds of the abbey and he formed a partnership with John Smithwick in 1710.

The brewery (now owned by Guinness) is the oldest in Ireland and, as it has grown, has gradually surrounded the ruins of the abbey, which still stand today. The image of the abbey is used on beer labels.

TASTING NOTES

■ **Smithwick's Draught (3.5% abv)**
Made with pale malt, roasted barley, maltose syrup, and Challenger, Goldings, Northdown and Target hops, this is a burnished amber-coloured ale with a generous head of foam. A creamy, malt, yeasty aroma is followed by a malty palate with a hint of dark fruit, with a short bitter-sweet finish. Stronger versions of this beer, at 4% and 5% abv, are brewed for export and are labelled either Smithwick's Ale or Kilkenny Irish Beer.

scotland

Medieval Scottish brewing was dominated by the Church. Today, the roots of monastic brewing in Scotland have all but disappeared, with just one or two breweries close to the border with England able to claim a link with the past.

evidence of extensive brewing by religious orders still survives in Scotland at Holyrood, Melrose, Banff and Dunbar. Unfortunately, the 16th-century Reformation led by John Knox blew away – often literally – many of Scotland's monasteries, and with them, their brewing traditions. The Catholic faith was driven underground and priests suffered great persecution. Today, only a few breweries continue to maintain Scotland's proud heritage.

Traquair House

Belhaven

Belhaven

Ale has been brewed at Belhaven, Dunbar, since the 12th century, when David I of Scotland granted the Isle of May in the Firth of Forth to Benedictine monks. In the centuries that followed, they colonized Fife and the Lothians, spreading not only the Gospel but also the art of brewing. The brothers who built the abbey at Belhaven enjoyed a fine reputation for their ale, produced from the well they dug and the cereals they grew in the carefully tilled soil. The land on which the Belhaven Brewery stands became known as Monks' Croft.

The monks were scattered as a result of the Reformation, but brewing on the site was not lost. Belhaven ale was supplied to the combined French and Scottish army that was quartered at Dunbar Castle for an invasion of England in the 1550s. Some of the vaults on the site today date from this period.

'THE BEST SMALL BEER I EVER HAD'
The brewery was bought by John Johnstone in 1719 and prospered to such effect that Belhaven's name became known not only in the Scottish Borders but further afield as well. Its products even found favour at the court of the Emperor of Austria, who remarked that Belhaven Ale was the Burgundy of Scotland. James Boswell, Dr. Johnson's biographer and companion and a man with a well-honed palate where drink was concerned, said Belhaven was 'the best small beer I ever had'.

■ **St. Andrew's Ale (4.5% abv)**

Brewed to commemorate Scotland's religious and military roots, and the long battle for independence from the English. The ale is brewed using pipkin pale malt, black malt, crystal malt, brewing sugar and Fuggles and Goldings hops. It is a deep ruby-red beer with a peppery hop aroma and tart gooseberry fruit notes. There is full nutty maltiness in the mouth, with a long, bittersweet finish finally dominated by the hops. The beer is dry hopped, meaning that a handful of hops is added to each cask as it leaves the brewery. It is the only Belhaven beer to get this treatment, which makes it unsually hoppy for a Scottish ale.

CONTACT

Belhaven Brewery Co Ltd • Monks' Croft
Dunbar • East Lothian EH42 1RS
Tel: 01368 862734 • www.belhaven.co.uk

TRAQUAIR
House Brewery Ltd

traquair house

Scotland's oldest inhabited stately home and a place of great beauty and tranquility, Traquair House has known turbulence and persecution over the centuries. It was first a simple heather hut built alongside a *quair* or stream that runs into the Tweed, the river that marks the border with England at what is now Innerleithen. In 1107, Alexander I signed a charter that placed the house under the control of the kings of Scotland. Eventually, the house was given to the nobility on the understanding that monarchs would have the right to frequent it. It was fortified in the 13th century in an unsuccessful attempt to keep out the English, who occupied the house, causing considerable damage.

RELIGIOUS PERSECUTION

The family that lived in the house were ennobled as the earls of Traquair in the late 15th century and were staunch supporters of the Stuart and Roman Catholic cause. John, the third Earl, was fined £500 (a vast fortune at the time) for marrying a Catholic. Mass had to be celebrated in secret, and a priests' hole, or hiding place, as well as an escape route for them were constructed. Members of the family were imprisoned, fined and isolated as a result of their beliefs. Mary Stuart, Queen of Scots, visited Traquair House: the rooms she occupied are open to visitors today. Bonnie Prince Charlie came to Traquair in 1745 to raise support for the Jacobite cause. When he left, the 5th Earl of Traquair closed the Bear Gates entrance to the grounds behind the prince, vowing that they would remain shut until a Stuart returned to the throne. They have stayed shut ever since.

THE BREWHOUSE REDISCOVERED

A house brewery was operating when Mary Stuart visited in 1566. In 1739, a huge copper was installed in the brewhouse beneath the chapel. The brewery then fell into disuse for more than 200 years. The 20th Laird, Peter

Maxwell Stuart, discovered the mash tun, open coolers and wooden stirring paddles when he was clearing out the brewhouse. He found that everything was in good working order and, with the energetic support of Sandy Hunter, the celebrated head brewer at Belhaven, started to brew again in 1965.

The rich, heady Traquair House Ale was at first only available to visitors to the house and at the nearby Traquair Arms Hotel in Innerleithen. But its fame spread and the bottled beer started to be exported to Japan, where it is a cult drink, as well as the United States. When the laird died in 1990, his daughter, Lady Catherine Maxwell Stuart, gave up a career in the theatre to run the house with her mother. She employs a professional brewer, but is active on the brewing and marketing side. She stages an annual beer festival every summer, to celebrate Scottish beer.

"From the bonny bells of heather
They brewed a drink Langsyne
Was sweeter far than honey
Was stronger far than wine"

ROBERT LOUIS STEVENSON
'heather ale'

TASTING NOTES

■ Bear Ale (5% abv)

There are rich malt and peppery hops on the aroma, with an underpinning of marmalade fruit. Dark, nutty malt and fruit dominate the palate, with a finish balanced between malt, fruit and hops, becoming dry with a spicy-peppery hop note.

■ Traquair House Ale (7.2% abv)

This is a dark and heady brew with stunning aromas of malt, peppery hops, dark chocolate, fruit and spices. There is a powerful vinous attack of malt and hops in the mouth with an intensely bitter finish and hints of pineapple and chocolate.

■ Jacobite Ale (8% abv)

First brewed in 1995 to commemorate the visit of Charles Edward Stuart 250 years earlier. The ale is spiced with ground coriander seeds and roasted grain. Herbal notes dominate the aroma, with spices, hops and rich malt in the mouth, and a tart, herbal and bitter finish.

CONTACT

Traquair House • Innerleithen • Peeblesshire EH44 6PP • Tel: 01896 830323
www.traquair.co.uk

north america

The United States and Canada are nations built upon immigration, and many of the early immigrants came from countries with long and powerful brewing traditions. Today, the micro-revolution has helped lead to a rediscovery of this heritage.

The history of brewing in North America stretches back to the Founding Fathers, and was augmented by the arrival of a 'second wave' of immigrants in the 19th century. Many of those who settled in the United States came from Central Europe, the heartlands of monastic brewing, and brought with them valuable beer-making skills. Canada, in contrast, is heir to a tradition that is primarily French, rather than German. Many settlers came from Flanders and Normandy, and their influence was an ale one, cross-pollinated by the beers of French-speaking Belgium.

Unfortunately, Prohibition intervened. With the manufacture of alcohol banned, only the richest and most powerful breweries survived. With the mass market to themselves, they concentrated on ever-blander and fizzier versions of lager, made with large amounts of cheap cereals.

Since the 1970s, however, a brewing renaissance has brought diversity back to North American beer drinkers. Small 'micro-brewers' (see page 110) have started to fashion ales and lagers based on original recipes — including some dazzling interpretations of Belgian and German beers with monastic associations.

ommegang

Don Feinberg and Wendy Littlefield have had a long love affair with Belgium and its beers. They were inspired by a visit to the country in 1980 and started to import Belgian beers into the US. In 1997, with the active participation of the Belgian brewers Affligem, Dubuisson and Moortgat, they opened their Ommegang Brewery in Cooperstown, New York, to brew

Belgian-influenced, abbey-style beers. The custom-built brewery, designed along the lines of a Belgian abbey-cum-farmhouse, is on the site of a former hop farm: this part of New York State was once a major hop-growing area.

The brewery takes it name from a great pageant first held for the Emperor Charles V in 1549 and still celebrated in Belgium today – the word *ommegang* is Flemish for 'walkabout'. The handsome brewery has been an enormous success from opening day, selling its bottle-fermented beers far and wide. Feinberg and Littlefield refuse to compromise on quality, despite pressure to brew more beer: the beers are matured slowly and lovingly on site before being bottled with their yeast, as the Belgian monastic beers are still brewed.

TASTING NOTES

■ **Abbey Ale (8.5% abv)**

A Burgundy-coloured ale with a deep collar of foam, a complex aroma of fruit, hops and spices, a palate rich in caramel, liquorice, toffee, chocolate and hops, and a dry finish in which citrus fruits, peppery hops and rich grain dominate. Made with pale and darker malts, and American and Belgian hop varieties.

CONTACT

Brewery Ommegang • New York Route 33
Cooperstown • New York 13326
Tel 800-656-1212 • www.ommegang.com

penn brewing

Tom Pastorius, who trained as a brewer in Munich for 12 years, is a direct descendant of the founder of the first German settlement in the US. The Penn brewery makes every effort to keep in touch with these roots, brewing fine German monastery-style beers. When Pastorius launched his brewery in 1989, he chose to base it in a restored 19th century German brewery complex in the steel town of Pittsburgh, where the workers have prodigious thirsts. He also hired a brewmaster trained at the renowned brewing faculty of Weihenstephan (see page 63), near Munich, itself once the site of a great monastery brewery.

Penn Brewing produces close to 20,000 barrels a year from an impressive plant based around hand-built copper vessels imported from Germany. Lagering takes place in horizontal tanks, which traditional Czech and German brewers believe give a slower second fermentation and a fuller palate to the finished beer. The beers adhere to the German Purity Law and are all-malt brews, with no cheaper cereal adjuncts.

CONTACT

Penn Brewing, 800 Vinial Street • Pittsburgh • Pennsylvania 15212
Tel 412-237-9402 • www.pennbrew.com

TASTING NOTES

■ Oktoberfest (5.6% abv)

A true amber-coloured March beer, with a juicy malt aroma balanced by tangy hops, a malty and nutty palate, and a dry finish with a good spicy hop note balancing the biscuity malt. Brewed with pale malt, caramalt, and American and German Hallertauer hop varieties.

■ St. Nikolaus Bock (8.4% abv)

A rich, dark beer made with pale, Munich, caramalt and dark malt, together with American and German Hallertauer hop varieties. There is a strong hint of roasted grain and chocolate on the aroma, full-bodied malt in the mouth with light hop notes, and a long finish dominated by roasted grain, chocolate and delicate hops.

stoudt's

Since the brewery opened in Adamstown in 1987, Stoudt's has built its reputation on the quality of its German-style beers, including Bocks. Carol Stoudt set up the brewery in the area known as 'Pennsylvania Dutch', a corruption of Deutsch, a reference to the German immigrants who settled there. Before branching out, Carol concentrated upon Bavarian-style beers and made an extensive tour of classic German breweries. The Bavarian-style beers are all brewed to the strictures of the German Purity Law.

BELGIAN-STYLE ABBEY BEERS
Having gained her spurs with German-style beers, Carol turned her hand to making beers in the style of Belgian Trappist and abbey ales. She brews brilliant interpretations of the Belgian Doubles and Triples, and pays great attention to the right choice of malts and hops. In the Belgian monastic tradition, she uses candy sugar for colour, flavour and to encourage a powerful fermentation. The ales are all available in bottle-conditioned form.

TASTING NOTES

■ Abbey Double (7% abv)
A deep bronze-russet beer with a rich malt and spicy hop aroma, a full malty palate, and a herbal note dominating the long finish. Brewed with five malts including pale, Munich and crystal malt, and four German Hallertauer hop varieties.

■ Abbey Triple (9% abv)
An orange-coloured beer with a spicy hop and rich malt aroma, a warming malt body rich in alcohol, and a big, lingering finish with spicy hops, fat malt and tart fruit. Both the Abbey beers are fermented with a Belgian yeast culture.

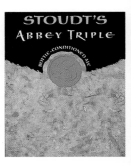

■ Anniversary Double Bock (7% abv)
A garnet-coloured beer with an enticing aroma of ripe malt and tangy hops, a firm malty body with a good hop balance, and a juicy malt and spicy hop finish. Brewed with caramalt, pale and Munich malts, and German Hallertauer hop varieties.

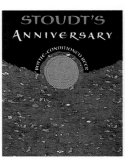

CONTACT
Stoudt's Brewing • Route 272 • PO Box 880 • Adamstown • Pennsylvania 19501
Tel 717-484-4387 • www.stoudtsbeer.com

MICRO-BREWERIES

A brewing revolution has taken place in Britain and North America, restoring choice and diversity, and helping to revive interest in long-forgotten beer styles. It is thanks to the passionate work of the micros that drinkers can taste the true flavours of monastery-style brews such as wheat beers, Bocks and March beers. Since many micros are attached to restaurants and bars, they can also be the perfect place to taste the beers and observe the brewing process.

Micro-breweries – micros for short – are small breweries with a limited output: the amount of beer produced could be as little as five barrels a week or as much as 5,000. The small brewery revolution started in the US, but it was inspired by the work in Britain of the Campaign for Real Ale (CAMRA). In the early 1970s, beer lovers formed CAMRA in an attempt

REVIVING TRADITIONAL BEER STYLES

The micro-brewing revolution has played a central role in the resurrection of lost and forgotten beer styles, creating beers which are closer in style to traditional monastery-brewed beers than to their bland mass-market rivals.

North American craft brewers have played a vital role in restoring genuine Bavarian Märzen beers. In Munich, this great style – brewed in March and traditionally tapped at the Oktoberfest – has largely disappeared, replaced by paler Oktoberfest beers, matured for shorter periods. The micros also offer a good range of German-style Bock beers, ranging from pale Maibocks to more robust darker Bocks meant for autumn and winter drinking, and dark and pale versions of German-style wheat beers now abound.

In Britain, revivalist micro-brewers have tended to concentrate on such indigenous styles as India Pale Ale, porter and barley wine. But the success of imported wheat beers from Belgium and Germany has prompted many of them to fashion beers made from wheat as well as barley.

to save Britain's unique beer style: cask-conditioned ale. Americans of a like mind who 'crossed the pond' returned home determined to restore good beer to their country. The micros helped to introduce North American drinkers to styles of beer that the big breweries had ignored, such as monastery-style beers previously available, if at all, only as imports.

Micro-breweries come in all shapes and sizes. Many American small breweries have custom-built brew houses with gleaming copper vessels. Other brewers make do with what they can find. Even unwanted farming and dairy vessels can be adapted, cut down and re-welded. Regardless of size and appearance, the success of the micros in both countries can be measured by their number. The United States, with 1,300 breweries, now has more beer producers than Germany, the world's greatest beer-drinking country. Britain, with only a fraction of America''s population, has more than 400 micros.

SMALL IS BEAUTIFUL

Micros are difficult to define on size alone. Just as important is a philosophy of care and attention to detail, which is not always present in the larger breweries. Many small breweries have been set up as labours of love rather than as purely commercial operations. Instead of using cheap cereal adjuncts, sugar and chemical additives to manufacture beer as quickly and cheaply as possible, micros place an emphasis upon beer made slowly and lovingly from natural ingredients.

TASTING

Some micro-breweries organise beer tastings or allow visitors, but this is quite unusual. Brew-pubs are a different proposition: they are open to the public, and to encourage the enjoyment of their beers, some offer a taste of the full range in small glasses. Micro-breweries that have restaurants attached – now a common feature in the United States – often offer special beer menus with tasting notes for each beer, and recommend dishes that are complementary.

OBSERVING

As well as producing better-tasting beer, another advantage of a micro plant is that the brewing process can be followed easily. Brew-pubs allow you to follow the process from the the comfort of your seat, while you enjoy the very beer that you see being brewed. Great skill goes into brewing, but it need not be a mystery. Not only have micro-breweries been instrumental in preserving traditional beer styles, they have also been at the forefront in developing new styles, such as pale, spritzy and hoppy summer beers. Seeing the process at first-hand can only add to the appreciation of the finished product.

sudwerk

The inspiration behind the Sudwerk Privat-brauerei Hübsch is clear: it was established in 1990 with the intention of bringing a taste of traditional Bavarian-brewing to the US. Sudwerk is the German for brewhouse – the impact of German brewing in the US can be measured by the fact that a widespread slang word for beer is 'suds' – while Hübsch means 'pretty'. Hübsch is also the founder's mother's maiden-name: it was his mother's stories of the wonderful beer halls in her native country that first inspired him to set up the brewery.

Sudwerk brews a number of beers in the German tradition, including a Bavarian-style unfiltered wheat beer, and seasonal beers such as a Maibock and a Märzen – a traditional Oktoberfest beer. The rich and nourishing Doppelbock, in particular, is reminiscent of the traditional winter beers brewed by Bavarian monks. The brewery imports malts and hops from Bavaria, and uses a yeast from Weihenstephan (see page 63), site of the world's oldest monastic brewery.

TASTING NOTES

■ Märzen (5.2% abv)
Made with five malts, and Hallertauer and Tettnanger hops, this is a true amber-coloured Munich-style March beer. Rich malt and tangy hops on the aroma and palate are followed by a big finish balanced between juicy malt and spicy hops.

■ Maibock (6.5% abv)
A copper-coloured beer with nutty malt and spicy hops on the aroma, full chewy and nutty malt in the mouth, and a big finish with creamy malt and tart, bitter hops. Brewed with caramalt, pale, Munich and roasted malt, and Tettnanger hops.

■ Doppelbock (7.1% abv)
Made with pale and chocolate malts and Hallertauer and Tettnanger hops. A deep copper-coloured beer with a massive aroma of roasted malt and chocolate that carries through to the palate, followed by a chewy malt, chocolate and light-hop finish.

CONTACT

Sudwerk Privatbrauerei Hübsch • 2001 Second Street • Davis • California 95616
Tel 916-925-8752 • www.sudwerk.com

UNÍBROUE

Unibroue is one of the great brewing successes of Canada. It was founded in 1990 with the aim of brewing Franco-Belgian type beers of the highest quality, and was advised in its early years by the Belgian breweries Liefmans and Riva. The company now brews a powerful, triple-fermented ale called La Fin du Monde, inspired by the Belgian Trappist Triples – the rich, spicy ales first brewed by the monks to drink on religious holidays.

The brewery has been sufficiently successful to open breweries in both the United States and France, and even sells the beers inside Belgium.

TASTING NOTES

■ La Fin du Monde (9% abv)

A pale gold beer with a powerful aroma of tart citrus fruit, spicy hops and rich malt, followed by a full-bodied malty palate balanced by spicy hops. At first, the long finish is dominated by rich malt, but it becomes dry, bitter, hoppy and fruity. Made with Belgian and German hop varieties, and pale Pilsner malt.

CONTACT

Unibroue • 80 des Carrières Chambly • Quebec J3L 2H6 • Tel 514-658-7658
www.unibroue.com.

2

enjoying beer

This chapter gives you all the essential information on serving, tasting and enjoying heavenly beers in the home. It's packed with practical advice, ranging from tips on how best to store the delicate beers successfully through to the best way to serve and bring out their full flavours. The tasting section describes how to appreciate fine beers, allowing them to breathe, and savouring the subtle complexities of the brew. And for a more complete sensory experience, the chapter contains some mouth-watering recipes, with step-by-step instructions on how to combine the flavours of monastery beers with delicious regional dishes.

serving Beer

From the choice of glass to the drama of the 'theatre of the pour', beer should be served in a way that will both please the tastebuds and seduce the eye.

temperature

Temperature is all-important. Many brewers put a recommended serving temperature on the bottle label. This is especially true of Belgian Trappist and abbey beers, where brewers take great pride in their work and want you to enjoy their beers in peak condition.

Storing beers

Bottled beer should be kept cool, and stored away from strong light, sunlight in particular. Most brewers put beer in brown or green bottles, which helps protect the liquid from the light, but strong light may cause the beer to develop unpleasant flavours similar to oxidation.

Most bottled beers can be stored flat, but those that contain a yeast sediment should be stored upright. If the beers are laid flat, not only will the sediment be dispersed and make the beer cloudy, but the natural carbonation produced during bottle fermentation will cause the beer to gush and foam messily when the top is removed.

ALE

It is a myth that ales, in particular British draught ales, should be served 'warm'. The recommended serving temperature for ale is 11-12°C. A degree or two warmer is acceptable, but below 11°C the beer may develop a 'chill haze' and look unacceptably cloudy in the glass. Ale served too cold won't be able to develop its aroma and flavour. The only exceptions are strong barley wines and old ales: as a result of their powerful fruity and often vinous flavours, they can be served at room temperature.

LAGER

The recommended serving temperature for lager is 6-8°C. Some light American or Australian lagers are served even colder: as they have little malt or hop character, the low temperature will not affect their flavour. But the rich and often powerful monastery-style lagers described in this book should not be stored at exceptionally low temperatures. Lagers served too warm take on syrupy characteristics that ruin the refreshing nature of the style.

Draught Beer at home

If you plan to hold a beer-tasting with friends, or merely wish to sample the pleasures of a strong, sipping winter ale or lager over several days or weeks, a draught container can offer beer at its best and most fresh. There are a few different types available.

KEG BEER

Before being run into the keg, the beer is filtered, artificially carbonated and usually pasteurised. This makes keg beer convenient and consistent, but also means that keg beers lack many of the flavours and subtleties retained in cask-conditioned beers, where the taste is allowed to mature in the cask.

CASK BEER

Run directly from fermentation tanks into casks, the beer is allowed to develop naturally, with a sediment of live yeast. The only gas is the natural gas produced during fermentation. This cask-conditioned beer can develop a complexity and flavour rarely found in the filtered, pasteurised keg beer. Casks need to be 'stillaged' — placed on their bellies so that the rear end is higher than the front — and then tapped and vented. This requires knocking a serving tap into a bung hole at the front, and a soft wooden peg into a second hole on top of the cask to allow the beer to vent off some of its natural gas. The beer has to stand for at least

a day to allow the yeast sediment to settle. Once a cask has been broached, it must be drained within a few days as it will slowly oxidize.

POLYPINS

Similar to a large, plastic wine box, Polypins are a type of cask. Smaller than the traditional large metal casks, they are also easier to set up and use. The beer has to settle for 24 hours but is then served by opening a tap — no separate taps or venting pegs are required.

the glass

In a purely sensuous way, the glass shape can influence the taste as well as the appearance. A glass like the large brandy goblet that goes with the Belgian ale Duvel is designed to cope with a beer that throws a vast head of foam, while the large bowl and tapering rim help amplify and condense the aroma. You may be lucky enough to have one of the glasses that has been specially designed to accompany the beer you are drinking, but it is by no means essential. It is perfectly acceptable to use any suitable glass container in your home: a conventional beer glass, or a large wine or brandy glass.

Whatever you use, it must be scrupulously clean and, above all, it should contain no residue from cleaning agents. If you take a glass from a dish washer, rinse it thoroughly under running cold water. Washing up liquids and detergents will not only leave a vile taste in the glass, but will kill the head on the beer.

Opening the bottle

Bottle-fermented beers should be allowed to breathe for a few minutes when the tops are removed. This allows some of the natural carbon dioxide to vent off. If the beer is too gassy, it will have an unwanted prickle on the tongue, and will mask the important malt and hop notes of the beer. On the other hand, don't leave beer without a stopper for too long: it will lose all its carbonation – what brewers call its condition – and will become flat and lifeless.

POURING TIPS

■ Hold the glass and bottle at eye level. Slowly pour the beer into the glass, raising the glass from the horizontal to the vertical as it fills. Let the beer trickle down the side of the glass.

■ When the glass is two-thirds full, raise it to the vertical and pour more quickly. This should give the required healthy head of foam. Don't pour the beer too slowly or the head will fail to materialize.

Pouring the Beer

The 'Theatre of the Pour' is how brewers and professional beer tasters describe the passage of beer from pump or bottle into the glass. The drama is in the way in which the beer swirls and eddies, looks turbid for a while, and then slowly separates into crystal-clear beer and inviting white head. Too many people merely plonk a beer glass on a table and up-end the beer into it so that the glass contains more froth than beer. This ruins the appearance of the beer and destroys the balance, knocking the vital hop aromas and bitterness out of solution.

Many monastery-style brews maintain the tradition of allowing yeast to remain in the bottle, so that the beer continues to develop after bottling. When pouring a beer containing

yeast sediment, hold the bottle at eye level, and stop pouring just before the yeast leaves the bottle. If some of the yeast does get into the glass, don't worry: it will do you no harm and is full of healthy nutrients.

If you are pouring a German wheat beer, you cannot avoid the yeast sediment getting into the glass. It's meant to be served that way. A German beer waiter will deliberately rotate the bottle as he or she pours, and will give a final dramatic roll of the bottle to ensure all the yeast enters the glass.

tasting Beer

Whether you are drinking for pleasure or taking part in a tasting, taking the time to fully savour the beer will help you to appreciate all the subtle distinctions of aroma, taste and texture.

There is no great mystique involved in beer tasting: the most important thing simply is to appreciate the aromas and flavours of the beer. The steps of the tasting process are merely intended to help you to focus more clearly upon the nuances and the complexity of the beer. Above all, enjoy!

IN THE GLASS

Begin by examining the colour of the beer. A true Irish Dry Stout, for example, should be jet black with just a tiny hint of ruby around the edge when held against the light, while many beers called India Pale Ale are too dark. Clarity is important in some styles, while even in more cloudy styles such as the German wheat beers, the liquid should always look appetizing. Swirl the glass to help appreciate the texture of the beer.

ON THE NOSE

Swirl the glass a little to release the aromas, and take a deep sniff. The aromas can tell you as much about the layers of flavour and the complexities of the beer as the taste itself. Depending on the style, you will detect malty and hoppy aromas plus possibly a fruitiness from either the hops or as the result of the natural chemical esters — the aromatic compounds created during fermentation.

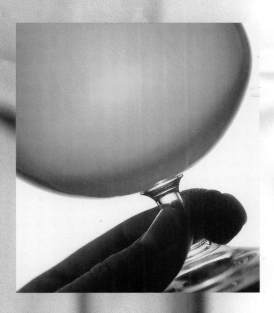

ON THE PALATE

Roll the beer around the mouth and over the tongue. As the beer passes over the tongue, you will detect more malt, hop and fruit notes. Different parts of this highly sensitive organ register the layers of sweetness, bitterness and saltiness in the liquid.

ON THE FINISH

Finally, let the beer slip down the back of the tongue and throat to appreciate the aftertaste or 'finish'. This is an important part of the tasting process, as a beer that starts malty on the aroma may finish with a pronounced degree of hop bitterness, or vice versa.

BEER TASTING TIPS

■ You may like to use tasting sheets with the names of each beer and with columns that allow the tasters to give marks out of ten for appearance, aroma, palate, finish and adherence to style.

■ You will need a good supply of glasses. If you reuse glasses, rinse them thoroughly between beers.

■ You should also have a good supply of uncarbonated mineral water to hand to drink between beers, plus plates with crackers or other kinds of dry biscuits to further cleanse the palate.

■ Many tasters like to have small squares of cheese as well, but these should be of the mild variety, as the likes of Blue Stilton or Mature Cheddar are too over-powering, especially if you are tasting delicately flavoured beers.

■ You should only taste one style of beer in a tasting: there is little point in attempting to match, say, pale Pilsners with English barley wines. Using the beers mentioned in this book, you could arrange tastings of Bocks, wheat beers, Belgian ales or English pale ales.

Beer and food

Whether in the kitchen or on the dining table, beer is the perfect accompaniment to a wide range of delicious dishes.

For centuries, beer was a constant companion at the dining tables of rich and poor alike. Before water was safe to drink, beer was a vital part of people's diet, providing essential nourishment as well as refreshment. The rapid growth in the consumption of wine in the 20th century tended to sideline beer, or reduce it to a liquid companion for a pub lunch. But the revival of interest in beer and its varied and distinctive styles has created a renewed interest in its role in kitchen and dining room alike. The Belgians, who take their beer seriously, have developed a *cuisine à la bière*, marrying their great malt beverages with dishes created by some of the country's leading chefs.

We may find it hard to emulate the more ambitious of these dishes, but we can create tasty meals using beers in this book. The Orval monastery, in Belgium, has produced a book of recipes, with simple, nourishing dishes that reflect the monks' simple lives. Their recipes naturally use the one beer they make: a full-flavoured, amber beer which blends beautifully with other ingredients. If Orval is not available, use a similar pale Trappist or abbey beer.

gratinéed onion soup

Serves 6

10 red onions

2 carrots

2 potatoes

1 large knob of butter

Salt, pepper and thyme

1 teaspoon sugar

1 bottle Orval beer

1 litre water

3 slices of wholemeal bread

6 slices of Port-du-Salut cheese

- Peel the onions, carrots and potatoes, and chop into fairly large pieces. Place in a food processor and chop finely.
- Put the knob of butter in a pan and heat. Add the vegetables without letting them brown. Season with salt, pepper and thyme, and add the sugar.
- Add the beer and water.
- Bring to the boil and leave to simmer for 20 minutes.
- Cut each slice of bread into quarters. Remove the rind from the cheese and cut into quarters.
- Place two quarters of bread in each of six oven-proof bowls. Pour over the soup and add one slice of cheese.
- Brown under the grill.

mussels cooked in beer

Serves 4

5 sticks celery

1 carrot

1 onion

1 bottle Orval beer

Pepper

4 kg mussels

- Carefully wash the mussels under running water.
- Dice the celery, carrot and onion.
- Place the chopped vegetables in a saucepan. Pour in the beer. Season with pepper.
- Bring to the boil and cook on medium heat for 5 minutes.
- Add the mussels and raise the heat. Shake the pan twice.
- Cook until the mussels open (discard any that do not) and serve in their shells with a little of the cooking juices.

glossary

abv Alcohol by Volume. The international method for measuring and declaring the strength of beer, and the method used throughout this book. In the US, a system known as Alcohol by Weight is also used, but many North American brewers now also declare strength in abv.

Abbey beer Commercial beers – made principally in Belgium – that may be brewed under licence from monasteries, although some have no monastic links whatsoever. Not to be confused with Trappist beers. Abbey beers are labelled *Abbaye* (French) or *Abdij* (Flemish).

Ale The world's oldest beer type, produced by warm or top fermentation. The term covers such styles as mild, bitter, porter, stout, old ale and barley wine, as well as abbey and Trappist ales and some types of Bock.

Aroma The 'nose' of a beer that gives an indication of the malty, hoppy and possibly fruity characteristics to be found in the mouth.

Beer Generic term for an alcoholic drink made from grain.

Bière de Garde French 'keeping beer', a style associated with French Flanders, first brewed by farmers in spring and stored to refresh their labourers during the summer months, but now produced all year round.

Bitter A draught English pale ale that may range in colour from gold through amber to copper. The name indicates a generous amount of hop bitterness.

Blond/blonde Term used in mainland Europe to indicate a light-coloured beer. The term is often used when a brewery produces brown and pale versions of the same or similar beers, as in the case of Leffe Blonde and Brune.

Bock German term for a strong beer, which can be either pale or dark, usually lagered for several months. The term is associated with the 'liquid bread' beers brewed by monks to sustain them during Lent. In the Netherlands, the term is sometimes spelt Bok, and beers there may be warm-fermented.

Bottle-conditioned/bottle fermented A beer bottled with live yeast that allows the beer to mature, gaining condition and extra alcohol, after bottling.

Brew-pub A pub that brews beer on the premises, usually for consumption only on the premises.

Brune A brown beer: see blond.

Cask ale Also known as cask beer or real ale. A draught beer that undergoes a secondary fermentation in the cask in the pub cellar, reaching maturity as a result of natural processes.

Doppelbock Extra strong type of Bock, usually around 7.5% abv or more, but not – despite the name – twice the strength of an ordinary Bock.

Draught Beer Served from a bulk container and drawn to the bar.

Dubbel Flemish word for double, first coined by the Westmalle Trappist brewery to indicate a strong dark ale of around 6.5% abv.

Dunkel German word meaning dark, indicating a lager beer in which colour is derived from well-roasted malts.

Enkel Dutch word for single, used to indicate a beer of modest strength, as in La Trappe Enkel.

Finish The aftertaste of a beer, the impression left at the back of the tongue and the throat.

Grand Cru A term given to the finest beer of a brewery, one thought to typify the house style. Usually used by Belgian brewers.

Gruit Medieval method of adding a blend of herbs and spices to beer.

Hefe German for yeast.

Helles German for light, indicating a pale beer, either lager or wheat beer.

IBU International Units of Bitterness, a scale for measuring the bitterness of beer.

IPA Short for India Pale Ale, the first pale beer in the world, associated with Burton-on-Trent in the English Midlands in the 19th century. First brewed for soldiers and civil servants based in India, it spawned pale ale and bitter in England, and even inspired the first lager brewers of Austria and Germany.

Irish Red Ale Beer made with the use of crystal and, sometimes, roasted barley to give beer a red tinge.

Lager From the German *lagerung*, meaning storage. Following primary fermentation, beer is 'cold conditioned' in tanks where the temperature is held just above freezing. As the yeast settles at the bottom of the tanks, a slow secondary fermentation takes place, carbonation increases, and a clean, quenching, spritzy beer results, usually lacking the fruity flavours associated with ale.

Lambic Belgian beer made by 'spontaneous fermentation', using wild yeasts in the atmosphere. True lambics are confined to the area of the Senne Valley centred on Brussels. A blended lambic, using young and aged beers, is known as gueuze.

Maibock/meibock German or Dutch words for a strong, usually pale, lager brewed to herald the arrival of spring.

Märzen/March beer Traditional Bavarian lager brewed in March and stored until the autumn, when it is tapped at the Oktoberfest. It was inspired by the Vienna Red beers.

Micro-brewery A small brewery with a small staff, often just a couple of people, brewing batches of beer for local distribution. 'Micros' have been at the forefront of the craft beer revival, and many have recreated old beer styles and designed new ones.

Mouth-feel The sensation that beer and its constituent parts – malt, hops and fruity esters – make in the mouth. The tongue is a highly sensitive organ and can detect sweetness, sourness, saltiness and bitterness as the beer passes over it.

Oktoberfest beers Medium-strength lager beer brewed in Munich for consumption at the famous autumn beer festival.

Pilsner/Pilsener/Pils Originally a golden, hoppy lager brewed in Pilsen in Bohemia. A true Pilsner is usually around 4.5-5% abv. In Germany, many brewers either spell the word Pilsener or shorten it to Pils to avoid any suggestion their beers come from Pilsen. In the Czech Republic only beers from Pilsen can use the term.

Porter A brown (later black) beer first brewed in London early in the 18th century. Called 'entire butt' by brewers, it acquired the name of porter due to its popularity with street-market porters. The success of porter created the modern commercial brewing industry in England and later in Ireland. The strongest porters were known as stout.

Quadrupel A Belgian beer of exceptional strength but rarely four times a strong as other beers.

Reinheitsgebot The 1516 Bavarian 'Pure Beer Law' that lays down that only malted barley and/or wheat, hops, yeast and water can be used in brewing. Cheaper cereals and sugar are not permitted. The law now covers the whole of Germany, but export beers may not necessarily adhere to it.

Stout Once a generic English term for the strongest or 'stoutest' beer produced in a brewery. With the rise of porter in the 18th century, strong porters were known as stout porters. Over time, the term was shortened to just stout, indicating a strong, jet-black beer, made with highly-roasted malts and roasted barley and generously hopped. Most closely associated today with Ireland.

Trappist Beers of the ale family made in breweries controlled by Trappist monks in Belgium.

Tripel Strong, usually pale beer, associated with the Westmalle Trappist brewery in Belgium, but now widely used throughout the Low Countries.

Vienna Red Term for the first successful commercial lager beer brewed in Austria in the 19th century. It was a halfway house between the dark lagers of Munich and the golden lagers of Bohemia.

Wheat beer Known as *weizen* (wheat) or *weiss* (white) in Germany, *blanche* in French or *wit* in Dutch and Flemish. Beer made from a blend of wheat and barley malt. Wheat beers are members of the ale family and may be unfiltered and cloudy, or filtered and bright.

index

acknowledgements

The author wishes to thank the following for their help in writing this book:

In Great Britain: Rupert Ponsonby of R&R Teamwork; Rupert Thompson and Pip Laycock of Refresh UK; Simon Stone and Tim Sears of the Blue Anchor; George Wortley of St. Peter's Brewery; Frances Brace of Greene King; Jim Burrows of Brakspear; Dick Burge of Nethergate; Stuart Ross of Belhaven.

In Austria: Conrad Seidl, the Beer Pope.

In Germany: Christof Eckel and Dr Karl-Werner Adler of Lowenbrau; Dr Peter Urbanek, archivist of Spaten-Franziskaner-Brau; Dr Martin Krottenhaler of Weihenstephan.

In Belgium: Francois De Harenne of Abbaye de Notre-Dame d'Orval; Jan De Brabanter of the Belgian Confederation of Brewers.

Carroll and Brown would like to thank:

Orval Abbey and Nicole Darchambeau for their generous permission to use recipes from the book *Flavours from Orval*, available from Orval (www.orval.be).

Martin Kemp of the Beer Shop, 14 Pitfield Street, London N1 6EY (Tel: 020 7739 3701 Website: www.pitfieldbeershop.co.uk), for supplying beer and glasses for photography. The beer shop has an excellent range of Trappist and abbey beers.

Production: Karol Davies and Nigel Reed
Picture Research: Mirco De Cet

Picture credits: FC:Jules Selmes; 2:Getty Images; 4:Weihenstephan; 5:(TR)Weihenstephan; (BL)Getty Images; 6/7:Weihenstephan; 8:(L) Getty Images (RF); (R)AKG photo, London; 9(R)Getty Images (RF); 10:Ruggero Vanni /Corbis; 11:AKG photo, London; 12:Bill Howes/Frank Lane Pictures/ Corbis; 13:Nethergate; 14/15: Spaten; 16:Bettmann/Corbis; 17:Fine Art Photographic; 18:Pictor; 19:Jopenbier; 20: AKG photo, London; 21:AKG photo, London; 22/23:Weihenstephan; 25:Owen Franken/Corbis; 26/27:Chimay; 28/29:Orval; 30:Orval 31:Spaten; 32:Rochefort; 33:Achel; 34/35:Westmalle; 36:Westvleteren; 37:Mirco De Cet; 38:St Bernardus; 39/40:Leffe; 41:Grimbergen; 42:St Sylvestre; 43:(L)St Sylvestre; (R)Corbis; 44:Castelain; 45:Duyck; 46:La Choulette; 47:Bailleux; 49:La Trappe; 51:La Trappe; 52/53:Brouwhuis Maximiliaan; 54:Brand; 55:Corbis; 56:St Peter's; 57:Paulaner; 59:Bob Krist/Corbis; 60:Spaten; 61:Bettmann/Corbis; 62:Paulaner; 63/64:Weihenstephan; 65:(TR)Andechs;(B)Don Klosterman; 66:Green King; 68:Andechs; 69:Weltenburg; 70/71:Spaten; 73:Adam Woolfitt/Corbis; 74/75:Schlag; 77:(L)Schutzengarten; (R)Getty Images; 78:Chimay; 79:Penn Brewery; 81:Dave G Houser/Corbis; 82:Francis G Mayer/Corbis; 83:Mirco De Cet; 84/85Marston's; 86/87:Brakspear; 88:St Peter's; 89:Nethergate; 90:La Trappe; 91:Ommegang; 92/93:Theakston; 94/95:Blue Anchor; 96:Greene King; 97:(Inset)Green King;Marston's; 98:Celtic Brew; 99:Corbis; 100:Celtic Brew; 101:Smithwick's; 102:Belhaven; 103:(L)Belhaven;(R)Mirco De Cet; 104/105:Traquair House; 107:(L)Ommegang;(R)Jonathan Blair/Corbis 108:Penn Brewery; 109:Stoudt's; 110/111:Dave Bartruff/Corbis; 114/115:Getty Images; 116/121:Jules Selmes; E:Weihenstephan BC:(TL/TCR)Marston's;(TCL)La Trappe; (TR)Spaten